The Careful Eye

Grammar, Editing, and Proofreading Exercises

Donald E. Holmes

Humber College
of Applied Arts and Technology

TEP THOMPSON EDUCATIONAL PUBLISHING, INC.

To Marian

The Careful Eye

Editing and Proofreading Exercises

Donald E. Holmes

Humber College
of Applied Arts and Technology

TEP THOMPSON EDUCATIONAL PUBLISHING, INC.

Copyright © 1995 Thompson Educational Publishing, Inc.

1st edition 1991

All rights reserved. No part of this publication may be reproduced or transmitted in any form or by any means, electronic or mechanical, including photocopy, recording, or any information storage and retrieval system, without permission in writing from the publisher.

Requests for permission to make copies of any part of the work should be directed to the publisher.

Canada

14 Ripley Avenue, Suite 105
Toronto, Ontario
M6S 3N9

Tel (416) 766-2763 / Fax (416) 766-0398

Canadian Cataloguing in Publication Data

Holmes, Donald E.
 The careful eye: grammar, editing and proofreading

2nd ed.
ISBN 1-55077-067-5

1. English language - Composition and excercises.
2. English language - Grammar - 1950 -
Problems, exercises, etc.   3. Proofreading -
Problems, exercises, etc.   4. Copy-reading -
Problems, exercises, etc.   I. Title.

PE1413.H65 1995   808'.402   C95-930417-7
Main entry under title:
Careful Eye, The

Printed and bound in Canada.

1 2 3 4   98 97 96 95

Table of Contents

Dedication ii
Foreword ix
Standard Correction Symbols xi

Section I: Rules

Parts of Speech 14
    Nouns 15
    Verbs 17
    Pronouns 20
    Adjectives 22
    Adverbs 23
    Conjunctions 24
    Prepositions 25
    Interjections 25

Verb Tenses 26
    Present 26
    Past 26
    Future 26

Advanced Applications 27
Shall and Will 27
Tenses
    Present Perfect 29
    Past Perfect 29
    Future Perfect 29
    Progressive Tenses 30
    Emphatic Tense 30
Verbals 31

Punctuation

Periods 33
Periods and Quotation Marks Together 35
Question Marks 36
Exclamation Points 36
Commas 37
Semicolons 40
Colons 42
Dashes 43
Brackets 44
Quotation Marks 44
Parentheses 45
Italics 46

Hyphens 47
Apostrophes 49

Its, It's, and . . . Its' 52

Sentence Patterns 55
Clauses
Simple 56
Compound 59
Complex 62
Compound-complex 65

Phrases
Prepositional 68
Participial 68
Gerund 68
Infinitive 68
Absolute 69

Section II: Exercises With Answers

Agreement 72
Comma splices 75
Comma splices, run-ons
   Career Foundations 76
Compound Sentences
   Dignified Dying 79
Sentence patterns 81
Run-ons, comma splices, commas
   Jean's Lessons in Learning 87
Phrases, clauses
   English: The key to jobs for immigrants 90
Apostrophes
   Without Advertising 93
Commas
   Mumbo-jumbo on Currriculum 96
Pronoun Antecedents
   Save the Roaches 98
Person Shifts
   Retirement 100
Verbals
   Bohdan's Munch 102
   Speyside Fred 104
Sentence Construction 107
Sentence Codes Applied 110

Section III: Editing and Proofreading

Level I

Fragments
- *Hammacher* ... 114
- *Telecommunicators* ... 115

Run-ons
- *P.E.I. Village* ... 116

Parallelism ... 117
General Editing ... 123
The Great Mistake Hunt ... 123
1. *The Beatles* ... 123
2. Run-ons and comma splices ... 124
3. Misplaced modifiers ... 125
4. Dangling modifiers ... 126
5. Faulty Pronoun references ... 128
6. Faulty Parallelism ... 129
7. Number, person, tense ... 131
8. Question marks, exclamation points, quotation marks, periods ... 132
9. Semicolons and colons ... 133
10. Commas ... 134
11. Apostrophes ... 135
12. Apostrophes: *Randy and Elizabeth's Cottage* ... 136
13. Plurals and Possessives: *The Zabans* ... 137

Punctuation and Pronouns: *This is Spinal Tap* ... 139
Fragments: *Dressing in Style* ... 142

Level II

Sentence variety, Diction
- *On-The-Job Performance* ... 144

Hyphens, Commas
- *Mrs. Grabbenclutch* ... 147

Verbals
- *Chivalry is Dead* ... 149

Spelling, Diction, Fragments
- *Death Trap I* ... 153

Fragments, Wrong words, Spelling
- *Death Trap II* ... 155

Mechanics, Spelling, Punctuation
- *Death Trap III* ... 158

Mixed punctuation, Diction
- *Proper Spelling* ... 160

Tenses, Punctuation, Diction
- Review of *This is Spinal Tap* ... 162

Punctuation, Spelling, Logic
- *Dangerous Dream World* ... 165

Agreement, Tenses, Punctuation
- *Guitar Concerto* ... 168

Punctuation, Word Choice, Person Shifts
 Tough and Athletic 170
Style, Editing
 A Qualified Secretary 172
Verbs, Agreements, Fragments, Comma splices, Logic
 Cars and Personalities 173
Capitalization, Punctuation
 News Release 175
Word Choice, Spelling, Agreement
 Impact of Language 178
Irregular verbs
 Humouresque 179
Grammar, Diction, Punctuation
 Valedictory Address I 180
Pronoun agreement, Diction, Tenses
 Valedictory Address II 182
Absolute modifiers, Adverbs, Correlative conjunctions
 Valedictory Address III 186

Subject Index 189

General Index 192

Foreword

The Careful Eye, Second Edition, is designed to help students succeed in college or university, as well as in the workplace. The concepts laid out here will enable you to control your own writing.

The Careful Eye is in three sections.

Rules, the first of the categories, presents the basics of grammar and punctuation to address the most common faults typically exhibited in first year, post-secondary students' writing.

Section two, **Exercises with Answers**, allows for practice of newly acquired grammatical skills by completing a series of exercises and then checking your answers against those provided. Should your answers differ from those provided, review the rules, and then consult an English teacher for further explanation. For most questions in this section, the answer is either right or wrong.

Editing and Proofreading, the third section, allows for more freedom in your answers--nonetheless, that is not total license to abandon all rules! In addition to the correct-incorrect answers of the former section, this latter one adds logic and diction. In essence, it focuses as much on editing as on proofreading, but the two skills are complementary.

In most cases throughout **The Careful Eye**, headings signal the principal errors; in the editing section, notwithstanding, you must think of the content and see what is written on the page. The headings guide you to some errors but are not a comprehensive list. As a result, the engaged reader will become both a meticulous proofreader and a critical thinker with a careful eye.

Whether for pleasure or for work, educated people acknowledge the interdependence of form and content. Ideas alone are insufficient in the modern workplace that expects accuracy, creativity and production from employees. People with full-time jobs and years of experience take grammar and editing courses to improve their writing, a skill that may not necessarily have been part of their jobs when they were hired. To this end, **The Careful Eye** presents a manageable condensation of grammar and punctuation to train you to be correct, clear, and effective in writing for a lifetime regardless of the situation. From the outset, you will work on sentences, those basic units of expression required in all prose. Grammatical explanations reveal how sentences are constructed. Sentences work like puzzles. Each sentence part is separate, yet it simultaneously affects all other parts surrounding it.

With only four sentence types at your disposal – simple, compound, complex, and compound-complex – you can learn the "codes" to create sentences with variety, which, in the final reading, reveal your control and flexibility with your own writing. By understanding sentence codes or components, you eliminate the haphazard approach to writing. "You know what I mean" and "anything goes" do not go. Writing, like working on a computer, works best if you learn the commands that allow you to produce the document. Applying those commands both systematically and repetitively consumes your time initially. It takes patience, but you can learn them. As you become familiar with the computer commands, you use them automatically, and the entire process is easier. In the same way, once you recognize the sentence parts and understand how they work in relation to other sentence parts, you have the knowledge to check for any "bugs" or errors in your work as well as in the work of others. This ability enhances creativity, builds self-esteem, and satisfies employers.

The exercises introduce you to standard, accepted terminology. Practising these exercises develops skill in an area of grammar that is precise. You learn the difference between what is grammatically correct and grammatically incorrect. Knowing this difference and having the ability to control your writing increase your ability for job promotion.

The Careful Eye focuses upon accuracy but not upon style. Principally, it emphasizes the single most important weakness demonstrated by students entering college--inaccuracy based on ignorance of what to do not because they cannot, but because they may never have been required to learn these skills. Now is no time to blame former teachers or educational systems, curricula, or even genetics. Adult, mature students can take charge of what they know and what they need to know. They accept this opportunity responsibly. It is an investment of money and time for your benefit. Gain the respect, not scorn, of your classmates and co-workers. Convert a present chore into a future pleasure.

Donald E. Holmes
Professor
Humber College of
Applied Arts and Technology
Etobicoke, Ontario

Standard Correction Symbols

ab	Faulty abbreviation
adj	Misuse of adjective
adv	Misuse of adverb
agr	Error in agreement
awk	Awkward construction
ca	Error in case form
cap	Use capital letter
con	Be concise
co-ord	Faulty co-ordination
cs	Comma splice
D	Error in diction
dev	Inadequate essay development
div	Incorrect word division
dm	Dangling modifier
emph	Emphasis lacking or faulty
exact	Inexact word
frag	Sentence fragment
fs	Fused sentence
g	Good use
gr	Error in grammar
hyph	Error in use of hyphen
inc	Incomplete construction
ital	Italicize or underline
K	Awkward construction
lc	Use lower case
log	Faulty logic
mixed	Mixed construction
mm	Misplaced modifier
mng	Meaning
ms	Incorrect manuscript form
no cap	Unnecessary capital letter
no ,	Comma not needed
no ¶	No new paragraph needed
num	Error in use of numbers
p	Error in punctuation
¶	Start new paragraph
coh	Paragraph not coherent
dev	Paragraph not developed
un	Paragraph not unified
pass	Ineffective passive voice
ref	Error in pronoun reference
rep	Unnecessary repetition
rev	Proofread or revise
run-on	Run-on sentence
shift	Inconsistency

Standard Correction Symbols (cont'd)

sp	Misspelled word
ss	Error in sentence structure
sub	Faulty subordination
t	Error in verb tense
U	Incorrect usage
var	Vary sentence structure
vb	Error in verb form
W	Wordy
ww	Wrong word
//	Faulty parallelism
x	Obvious error
^	Something missing
)	Move right
(	Move left
#	Insert space
=	Insert hyphen

Section I: Rules

Parts of Speech

In English, every word falls into one of the eight parts of speech depending on its use in a sentence. Therefore, words in a sentence may name people, places, things, ideas, and qualities (**nouns** and **pronouns**); they may express the action (**verbs**); they may modify (**adjectives** and **adverbs**); they may join parts of the sentence (**prepositions** and **conjunctions**); and, finally, they may be used to express mild or strong emotion (**interjections**).

A single word can be used as different parts of speech.

For example:
a. I **love** *(verb)* her.
b. **Love** *(noun)* is a beautiful thing.
c. The **love** *(adjective)* story is interesting.
d. She read **lovingly** *(adverb)*.
e. **Guard** *(verb)* the property.
f. The **guard** *(adjective)* dog was fierce.
c. The **guard** *(noun)* stood motionless.
d. The visitors drove through the city **guardedly** *(adverb)*.

Nouns

Nouns name the following:
a. people   (Andrea, Ms Smith, president, Scott)
b. places   (Toronto, college, island, Ukraine)
c. things   (computers, chairs, surfboards, rings)
d. qualities   (honesty, dependability, reliability, graciousness, integrity)
e. concepts   (love, hate, anger, hope, peace)
f. activities (cycling, reading, dancing, organization)

1. Common nouns,
used without capitals, name members of a class of people, places, or things.

> **carpet, book, stadium, student,
> prairies, paper clip, tape, glass,
> books, plant, grass, street, child**

2. Proper nouns
require capitals and name specific people, places, or things.

> **Alicia, *The Careful Eye*, SkyDome,
> Milton Born-with-a-Tooth, Santa Claus,
> Moncton, Grand Manan Island, Newfoundland, Kingston**

3. Concrete nouns
name objects that can be perceived by the senses.

> **computer, key, sand,
> apple, textbook,
> wine, puck, football, pencil**

4. Abstract nouns
name qualities or concepts not perceived by the senses.

> **ambition, love, hate, jealousy, co-operation,
> consideration, fairness, loyalty, strife,
> depression, anger, greed, intuition**

The Careful Eye

5. Collective nouns
identify groups.

**jury, committee, faculty, class, union,
team, squad, assembly, audience, department,
congregation, group, staff, administration**

NOTE: Mass nouns are not made plural for they name things that cannot be easily counted: dust, peace, tranquility. Many of them are also classed as either collective or abstract nouns.

6. Gerunds
are verb forms that act as nouns.

**walking, dancing, sewing, thinking,
managing, management, reading, playing,
studying, writing, hoping, working, wishing**

NOTE: A gerund must be used after the following verbs:

admit, anticipate, avoid, consider, defer, delay, deny, detest, dread, enjoy, excuse, fancy, finish, forgive, imagine, involve, keep, mind, miss, pardon, postpone, prevent, recollect, resent, resist, risk, save, stop, suggest, understand

1. Geraldine admits having written the letter.
2. We anticipate being involved in the fundraising event.
3. Please avoid misplacing the application if you intend to apply for the grant.
4. Keep reminding yourself of how important study is; it involves recollection and comprehension under stress.
5. Resist touching the electric wires, mixing with the wrong group, and bowing to peer pressure.

Verbs

Verbs are the most important words in a sentence; they express the action or the state of being.

> He wrote a letter. *(action)*
> They were in the theatre. *(state of being)*

Verbs are **transitive** where they need a direct object to complete their meaning, **intransitive** where they require no direct object because the meaning is complete with the verb, or **linking** where they express the relationship between the subject and the complement of the subject.

In the examples that follow, locate the verb and ask one of these two questions: **what** or **whom**? If you get an answer to one of these questions–the direct object – the verb will be transitive.

1. The florist cut the gladiolus. *(direct object)*
2. The secretary typed the letter. *(direct object)*
3. The man telephoned his lover. *(direct object)*

Locate the verbs in the following sentences, but note that you'll not get an answer to one of the previous questions – **what** or **whom**. Since there is no direct object to receive the action, these verbs are **intransitive**.

1. The plumber worked.
2. The opera star sang in the concert hall.
3. I lay in the sun yesterday.
4. She exercised for three hours!
5. They argued during the intermission.

Linking verbs (also known as copulative verbs) express the relationship between the subject and its complement. Generally, they are easily recognized because they are often forms of the verb **to be** or they are one of the senses. The most common of them are the following:
**is, am, was, be, become, appear,
seem, taste, smell, sound, look,
feel, grow,** and **prove.**

1. Her name **is** Morag.
2. She **grows** an inch each month.
3. The purse **seems** inexpensive.
4. The opera singer **looked** composed in the Ford Centre for The Performing Arts.
5. They **became** political during intermission.

The Careful Eye

The Careful Eye

Occasionally, verbs are considered to be **auxiliary**; that is, they help other main verbs form different tenses. Chief among the list of auxiliary verbs are the following:

**am, be, is, is able to,
was, were, can, did, do, does,
had to, have, may, might,
must, ought to, shall, should,
should have, should have been,
used to, will, will be, will have,
would, would have**

1. They **should** finish on time.
2. They **ought to** study for the examination.
3. Alicia **did** arrive on time for the last show.

Regular verbs usually have consistent forms with minimal change from one form to the other. Use their forms correctly. Consult a dictionary if necessary.

1. **Build, built, built**
2. **Tell, told, told**
3. **Walk, walked, walked**
4. **Work, worked, worked**

1. The contractors **build** houses.
2. The former owners **built** this addition to the deck.
3. We **have built** our own chalet.

Other verbs, however, form their principal parts irregularly. These verbs are referred to as **irregular** or **strong** verbs in the English language.

1. **Am, was, been**
2. **Bid, bade, bide**
3. **Blow, blew, blown**
4. **Hang, hanged, hanged (execute)**
5. **Hang, hung, hung (suspend)**
6. **Lie, lay, lain**
7. **Mistake, mistook, mistaken**
8. **Rise, rose, risen**
9. **See, saw, seen**
10. **Write wrote, written**

1. The strongest winds **blow** from the north.
2. The gentle wind **blew** from the south yesterday.
3. The wind **has blown** all morning.
4. **Hang** that prisoner.
5. The prisoner **hanged** himself.
6. The prisoner **was hanged** in the early morning.
7. Each day we **lie** down at noon.
8. Two naive beach-bums **lay** in the sun for the entire afternoon.
9. In the past, I **have lain** in the sun for hours; now, of course, I **lie** in the shade where I **lay** yesterday reading a good novel.

The Careful Eye

Pronouns

> Pronouns are words that replace nouns in sentences. They are divided chiefly into seven categories.
>
> 1. Personal
> 2. Relative
> 3. Demonstrative
> 4. Interrogative
> 5. Reflexive
> 6. Indefinite
> 7. Reciprocal

1. Personal

A. Subject pronouns (used as subjects or subject complements in sentences)

I, you, he, she, it, *(singular)*
we, you, they *(plural)*

B. Object pronouns (used as objects in sentences)

me, you, him, her, it, *(singular)*
us, you, them *(plural)*

C. Possessive pronouns (used to indicate ownership)

my, mine, your, yours, his, her, hers, its, *(singular)*
our, ours, your, yours, their, theirs *(plural)*

2. Relative
Relative pronouns connect a dependent clause to an independent clause.

who, whose, whom, which, that, whoever, whomever, whichever, whatever

3. Demonstrative
Demonstrative pronouns identify another noun or pronoun.

this, that, these, those, such

4. Interrogative

Interrogative pronouns introduce a question.

who, whom, whose, which, what, whoever, whichever, whatever

5. Reflexive

Reflexive pronouns refer to the subject of the clause or of the sentence. They are compounds of personal pronouns and the words "self" or "selves".

myself, yourself, himself, herself, itself, ourselves, yourselves, themselves

6. Indefinite

Indefinite pronouns are less specific in reference than most other pronouns. Frequently, it is difficult to locate the antecedent of them. Many of these pronouns are recognizable because of their endings – **one, thing, body**. Pronouns with such endings are **singular** and require singular antecedents as well as singular verbs.

all, another, any, anyone, anything, anybody, everyone, everything, everybody, some, someone, something, somebody, few, many, nobody, nothing, no-one, none, one, several, each

7. Reciprocal

Reciprocal pronouns show an interchange of action between people or things.

each other *(refers to two only)*
one another *(refers to three or more)*

Adjectives

Adjectives are used to modify a noun or pronoun by describing or limiting its meaning to make it more nearly exact. They are frequently – but not always – recognized by their endings.

*NOTE: The articles, **a**, **an**, and **the** are also adjectives.*

Friendly and **lovely**, although they end in **ly** and look like adverbs, are actually adjectives.

able	livable,	likable,	agreeable
al	hypothetical,	experimental,	impractical
ary	arbitrary,	customary,	pulmonary
en	golden,	flaxen,	rotten
esque	humouresque	picturesque	statuesque
ful	skilful,	dutiful,	healthful
ible	flexible,	irresistible,	compatible
ic	ironic,	historic,	phallic
ish	selfish,	boyish,	babyish
ive	festive,	responsive,	corrosive
less	loveless,	fearless,	mindless
ous	nervous,	jealous,	anxious
some	fulsome,	wholesome,	lonesome
y	risky,	tricky,	healthy

Adverbs

Adverbs are used to modify a verb, adjective, or another adverb. Generally, they answer such questions as how, when, where, why, how often, how much, to what extent, to what degree. The most recognizable ending is **ly** although others end in **wise** and **ways**

NOTE: Do avoid adding "wise" to nouns unnecessarily as in "moneywise" and "securitywise"; this colloqialism of the 1960s and 1970s is unacceptable in semiformal and formal writing.

ly	funnily, honestly, dutifully
wise	lengthwise, crosswise,
ways	sideways,

Common adverbs that do not take the **ly** form are these. They indicate time, place, extent, or degree.

again	**soon**	**almost**	**there**
always	**today**	**badly**	**tomorrow**
here	**every**	**never**	**well**
nor	**yesterday**	**now**	**not**

Adverbs: Special problems

Irregular adverbs change their form in this manner.

Positive	**Comparative**	**Superlative**
badly	worse	worst
ill	worse	worst
well	better	best

The positive helps to make one statement precise; the comparative is used to compare two things within a sentence; and, finally, the superlative is used to compare three or more items.

1. The wrestler performed badly today.
2. The skater acted worse today than yesterday.
3. Of the four options, the last proved to be the worst.

Conjunctions

Conjunctions are words that join words, phrases, and clauses in sentences. The three categories of conjunctions are **co-ordinating, subordinating,** and **correlative.**

1. Co-ordinating conjunctions
(often referred to as **FAN BOYS**)
join two independent clauses.

for	and
nor	but
or	yet
so	

2. Subordinating conjunctions
(used to begin dependent adverb clauses in complex and compound-complex sentences)

after	since	although	so that
as	though	because	unless
before	until	how	when
if	where	in order that	while

3. Correlative conjunctions
(a combination of subordinate and co-ordinate conjunctions correlating only two ideas)

both . . . and
either . . . or
neither . . . nor
not . . . but
not only . . . but also

The Careful Eye

Prepositions

Prepositions are words used to show the relationship of a noun or pronoun to some other word in a sentence. All prepositions require objects. Here is a list of the most commonly used prepositions.

about	above	across
after	against	along
alongside	amid	among
around	at	before
behind	below	beneath
beside	besides	between
beyond	but	by
concerning	despite	down
during	ere	except
excepting	for	from
in	in front of	inside
into	like	near
notwithstanding	of	off
on	on account of	onto
outside	over	per
regarding	save	since
through	throughout	till
to	toward	under
underneath	until	unto
up	upon	with
with respect to	within	without

Interjections

Interjections are words inserted into a sentence to convey mild or strong emotion. The strong interjection is followed by the exclamation point; the weak one, by the comma.

NOTE: Neither is for business writing; both are reserved for fictional and informal writing.

Oh, you don't say so?
Hurrah! The Leafs won!
Wow! What superb gymnastics.

Verb Tenses

Past, Present, and Future Tense

Tense is the change in the form of the verb to indicate the time of the action.

I. The present tense signifies present or habitual action or condition.

   1. They are working now.
   2. The employees are walking home.

II. The past tense indicates that action or condition occurred during some definite past time. This action has been completed before the present moment.

   1. He was walking home.
   2. They exchanged the gift yesterday.

III. The future tense indicates that action will occur in the future, but it has not begun yet.

   1. She will await your call.
   2. We shall go to Vancouver next month.

The **future tense** can also be expressed by a combination of the present tense and an adverb.

   1. I **am enrolling** in physics **tomorrow.**
   2. I **am going** to enrol in grammar **next week**.
   3. Her cousin arrives, **first thing in the morning.**

Advanced Applications

Shall and Will

> Shall and will are almost interchangeable in vernacular English; yet, in the written form of the language, the distinction is retained. The use is as follows for normal future tense.

I **shall**
You will
He will
She will
It will
We **shall**
You will
They will

> In the preceding list, **shall** is used with first person singular **I** and first person plural **we.** If, however, we wish to show strong determination, promise, or intention, both **shall** and **will** are reversed in their use. Compare the following list to the preceding one.

I **will**
You shall
He shall
She shall
It shall
We **will**
You shall
They shall

"I **will** meet you by the front door," implies that I'll meet you there regardless of the obstacles that may be placed in my way. Conversely, "I **shall** meet you at the front door" is merely a statement of fact indicating only that action will occur some time in the future.

"You **will** do your homework" expresses simple future tense; the homework will be done at a later time. "You **shall** do your homework" elicits promise; it is strong; the speaker is determined to complete the task or have it completed.

The Careful Eye

Exercises

Select the correct form indicated in brackets.

1. We (will, shall) have left by noon. *(Future)*
2. We (will, shall) have left by noon regardless of the weather. *(Determination)*
3. I (will, shall) write a letter to my father for Father's Day. *(Determination)*
4. You (shall, will) have time work on your own project. *(Future)*
5. It (will, shall) rain before I go white water rafting again. *(Future)*
6. He (will, shall) propose to her only if his mother gets a free ticket to Halifax. *(Condition)*
7. She (will, shall) accept his proposal provided that he be articulate in English. *(Condition)*
8. They (will, shall) study for their OACs in the spring. *(Future)*
9. You, too, (will, shall) rehearse all material in preparation for accreditation. *(Determination)*
10. If you eat a balanced diet, you (will, shall) dance more precisely and energetically. *(Intention)*

ANSWERS:

1. Shall;	*2. Will;*	*3. Will;*	*4. Will;*	*5. Will;*
6. Shall;	*7. Shall;*	*8. Will;*	*9. Shall;*	*10. Shall*

In questions, use the **shall-will** form expected in the answer to the question.

1. Will they come to the party? They will.
2. Shall we prepare lunch now? We shall.
3. Shall you go on the cruise? I shall.
4. Shall I show you my disposable contact lenses? I shall.

Use **should** with all persons to convey obligation.

1. I should fight for freedom.
2. You should lose some weight.
3. He should not argue with his parents.
4. She should be responsible for her decisions.
5. We should invite the Fords to dinner.
6. The manufacturers should honour our stove's warranty.

Present Perfect Tense

In this tense, "perfect" means completed, so the action began in the past and is now either completed or still occurring. To form this tense, use **has/have** and the past participle of the verb.

1. I have lived in Ontario since 1972.
2. Politicians have been discussing the constitution for over a decade.
3. It has been raining every weekend since May!

Past Perfect Tense

In this tense, the word "had" together with the past participle (normally ending in **ed, d, t,** or **en**) indicates action that began in the past and was completed in the past prior to another action.

1. She was annoyed because he had arrived late.
2. They moved to New Zealand by the time they had sold their house.
3. She argued that she had broken no law.
4. He admitted to Geraldo that he had been seeing Oprah.
5. The boy confessed that he had been swiping his grandmother's ginger cookies.
6. The student had chosen to attend college before his/her summer job ended.

Future Perfect

This tense uses a combination of the future tense of **have** and a past participle. It indicates that two actions will be completed in the future, but one of them will end before the other.

1. I shall have ended my examination by midnight.
2. Jill will have delivered her address to the Olympians by July 10.
3. We shall have invited them by the end of summer.
4. They will have been visiting us by Canada Day.
5. The judge will have been adjudicating us by noon on Labour Day.

The Careful Eye

Progressive Tenses

The progressive tense combines the present form of the verb **to be** with the present participle – ending in **ing** – of another verb.

1. I am building a deck.
2. He is bidding on the antique clock.
3. Henry is repairing his motorcycle.

The past progressive tense uses the past form of **to be** and the present participle of another verb.

1. He was skateboarding dangerously.
2. You were bidding on the antiques in the market.
3. Henry was repairing his motorcycle.

The future progressive tense uses the future form of the verb **to be** and the present participle of another verb.

1. We will be making plans shortly.
2. They will be exporting potatoes to Vermont in April.
3. Eleanora will be making costumes for Carabana in August.

Emphatic Tense

Only one verb, **to do**, can create the emphatic tense in English. It is used for additional emphasis or effect and for questions. To create the emphatic, add **do, did,** or **does** to the infinitive. Only the present and past emphatic can be created; no future exists with the emphatic.

1. Marc does wish to become bilingual. *(Present emphatic)*
2. They did try to behave properly. *(Past emphatic)*
3. I do intend to win a medal. *(Present emphatic)*
4. She does try to comprehend our customs. *(Present emphatic)*
5. Andrea and Kelly did agree to work harder. *(Past emphatic)*
6. Neither she nor I do intend to quit the course. *(Present emphatic)*
7. Either the women or the girl does pretend to use the computer effectively. *(Present emphatic)*
8. The newly hired professor does enjoy her teaching. *(Present emphatic)*
9. A senior administrator did refuse to accept his gift. *(Past emphatic)*
10. This pen does work after all. *(Present emphatic)*

Verbals

While they are derived from verbs, they themselves are not verbs, rather they are verb forms that act as nouns, adjectives, and adverbs.

1. Gerunds
are the verb forms ending in **ing** that function as nouns.

   a. Smoking is now an illegal habit in many businesses.
   b. He quit smoking.
   c. WordProcessing is Tara's hobby.
   d. Peter and Amanda enjoy skiing, especially in winter.

2. Infinitives
are the present form of the verb preceded by **to**.

   a. Try to phone me this evening.
   b. To be successful requires dedication and determination.
   c. Whenever I have the opportunity, I'll try to go shopping.

3. Participles:
Either past or present, participles function as **adjectives**; they describe nouns or pronouns, and they will have no helping verb accompanying them.

   a. I saw the teacher preparing a tax return.
   b. Having done all calculations correctly, the teacher claimed a refund.
   c. He saw the broken golf club.
   d. The burst balloon lay on the table.
   e. Screaming, the child left the theatre.

Exercises

In the following sentences, identify the participles that function as adjectives.

   a. Frank tied the torn curtain.
   b. He skidded on the cracked ice.
   c. Laughing, Alice ran to her dad.
   d. The old woman held out her withering hands to her granddaughter.
   e. She defeated a surprised candidate in the election.
   f. Two of his cherished characteristics remained with him: unbroken will and willing determination.
   g. The sleeping man snored loudly yet constantly.

The Careful Eye

> When an adjective follows linking verbs (forms of the verb **to be** and the senses), the adjective will be separated from the noun or pronoun it describes. The separation makes no difference to the description.

Locate the adjectives (complements) in the following sentences.

a. Adrian is quick.
b. Keith seems kind.
c. The grass appears healthy and strong despite the lack of rain.
d. The Rose of Sharon looks lovely in August.
e. Marian's car has been painted midnight blue.
f. The award-winning book is dull.

ANSWERS

a. quick;
b. kind;
c. healthy / strong;
d. lovely;
e. midnight blue;
f. dull

Punctuation

Periods

1. **Use a period after every statement, command, or request.**

   a. When I decided to return to college, it was for the sole purpose of acquiring skills that I would need when I re-entered the work force.
   b. This decision, in itself, was easy.

2. **Use a period after an initial or an abbreviation.**

   a. Mr., Mrs., M.D., M.P., Rev., oz., lb., etc.
   NOTE: Ms is not an abbreviation and does not require a period; however, for the sake of consistency in addresses, we frequently use a period after it.
   b. We received the c.o.d. package at 11:23 a.m.

3. **Use a period to punctuate numerals, especially to separate dollars from cents in monetary sums or to signal decimal fractions.**

   a. We paid $4.97 for the new disc.
   b. The Subaru Wagon has a fuel economy of 12.9 litres per 100 km. city, and 9.4 litres per 100 km. highway.

4. **Use a period following a letter or a number in a formal outline or report if the number or letter marks a division of material and if it is not enclosed in parentheses.**

   1. **Methods of classroom evaluation this semester**
      A. External examiner
      B. Student evaluation
      C. Teacher assessment

   2. **Formal report headings include**
      A. Abstract
      B. Summary
      C. Recommendations

The Careful Eye

> 5. Use a period after a nonsentence. A nonsentence (lacking subject and verb) is a legitimate unit of expression in fictional writing especially where dialogue is present; it is unacceptable in business writing. The nonsentence only serves to answer questions in dialogue.

1. **As a response to a question like "How are you?"**
   a. Fine.

2. **As a mild exclamation on its own.**
   a. Ouch.

3. **As a form of greeting.**
   a. Good morning.
   b. G'day.

NOTES:
1. *Commonly understood abbreviations such as RCMP, CBC, YMCA, YMHA, BMW, FBI, CAA, rpm, mph, need no periods following them.*

2. *The titles of reports and essays have no periods following them.*

3. *A nonsentence and a fragment are not the same. A fragment is an unintentional omission of either a subject or a verb – sometimes even both – from an idea; careful readers can easily distinguish nonsentences from fragments in the context of the discourse. No amount of defense makes fragments correct in business writing.*

Periods and quotation marks together

When the entire statement is quoted, the period ends the sentence and the quotation marks follow the period. In other words, when the entire sentence is quoted, the question mark goes inside the quotation mark. Conversely, if there are introductory words not included within the quoted portion of the sentence, the presence of that initial phrase or word dictates that the period will go outside the quoted portion so that the entire sentence is punctuated. In essence, the period applies to the entire sentence, not merely to the portion within quotation marks.

*NOTE: In **Great Britain**, periods and commas, colons and semicolons always follow quotation marks; in **The United States**, periods and commas are always inside quotation marks and semicolons and colons outside them. **Canada** has a mixture, so whatever your workplace requires, be consistent with the use throughout the entire document.*

1. The book review of Donald MacKay's **The People's Railway: A History of Canadian National**, comments quite rightly that "by the 1980s the trend (in railway diversification) was reversed, and the range of services has *[sic]* shrunk".
   – *The Financial Post, May 15, 1993.*

2. The reintroduction of parking meters will help Brampton. "But what we need here is a high-quality ladies wear shop and shoe store to generate business."
   – *Real Estate News, June 4, 1993.*

3. "We saw the potential of the downtown," Jonathan said.
   – *Real Estate News, June 4, 1993.*

The Careful Eye

Question Marks

1. Use a question mark at the end of a direct question.

   a. Do you know what the ozone reading is for today?
   b. What countries now border Zimbawbe?

2. Use a question mark to punctuate questions added to the end of statements.

   *NOTE: there **must be** a comma at the end of the statement preceding the question.*

   a. Saturday was a beautiful day, wasn't it?
   b. You do have a summer job, don't you?

3. Use a question mark to indicate doubt about a statement or fact.

   a. Jesus was born in 4 B.C. (?) in Bethlehem.
   b. There are two (?) creation stories in Genesis.

Exclamation Points

Use the exclamation point to express **strong** emotion.

   a. Impossible! Linus learned the windows command.
   b. Will that man ever stop complaining!

Commas

1. Use a comma to separate two independent clauses joined by a co-ordinating conjunction:
   for, and, nor, but, or, yet, and **so**.
   These conjunctions are remembered as "FAN BOYS".
   NOTE: The comma is necessary and does precede the conjunction.

   a. The teachers supported multiculturalism, yet they had no idea of how to achieve it in the classroom.
   b. The package arrived on time, but the contents were damaged.

2. Use a comma following an introductory dependent clause.

   a. After she had eaten the steak, she knew it had been undercooked.
   b. Because I have time to study today, I'll be prepared for the test.

3. Use a comma to separate **three** or more items in a series.
   NOTE: There is a comma before the "and" in a series of three of more items, except when the last two items are considered as one, the comma is omitted.

   ### a. Words in a series
   The children disliked broccoli, carrots, beets, and asparagus.

   ### b. Phrases in a series
   Newspapers are available on newsstands, in libraries, and by subscription.

   ### c. Clauses in a series
   (NOTE: This rule is not commonly applied in Canada)

   1. They read in the library, they studied in the park, and they completed the project successfully.
   2. They loved, they lived, they remained faithful.
      (NOTE: A more acceptable version is to use a semicolon following "library" in the first sentence.)

4. Use a comma to separate two or more co-ordinate adjectives of equal importance. No comma follows the second adjective.

   a. They climbed the crooked, treacherous trail.
   b. Aggressive, disruptive, impertinent behaviour is best displayed in solitude.

The Careful Eye

5. Use a comma to set off parenthetical expressions, words, or phrases that interrupt the flow of a single principal clause.

   a. Birthdays do, in fact, tell tales even on English teachers!
   b. Her house renovations, nonetheless, will be completed soon.

6. Use a comma to set off absolute phrases from the remainder of the sentence. (An absolute phrase consists of a noun and a participle that have no grammatical connection to the remainder of the sentence, yet the phrase is still part of its thought.)

   a. The bridge having collapsed, we went home.
   b. Our work finished, we went to the movie.
   c. That done, we went home.
   d. Marian edited and proofread the transportation reports, she being meticulous.
   e. All things considered, the employee received a good retirement package.

7. Use a comma to set off names or words used as names in direct address.

   a. Nancy, why are you fascinated with pigs?
   b. For an encore, ladies and gentlemen, I'll dance "Seann Triubhas".

8. Use a comma to set off **yes** and **no** at the beginning of the sentence.

   a. Yes, I paid my tuition fees.
   b. No, she has no idea where she left her keys.

9. Use a comma with **mild** interjections.

   a. Oh, I did not notice your wrist.
   b. Well, there is no need to decide on policy for another year.
   c. Sue, we will be there for the party.

10. Use commas to separate direct quotations from other words in the sentence.

    a. "You have my word," she said.
    b. She said, "You have my word".
    c. "You have my support," she said, "on whatever option you select."

11. Use a comma to set off expressions like **such as, especially, particularly,** and others expressing contrast and introducing only one or two items.

   a. He enjoys his courses, especially Introduction to Computers.
   b. During our spare time we take courses, such as Language 103 and Humanities, to keep us up-to-date.

12. Use a comma as a substitute for a missing or intentionally omitted word – normally a verb – that appears in the earlier part of the sentence.

   a. I attended Prince of Wales College; later, Acadia University.
   b. I attended Acadia University; my sister, Prince of Wales College.

13. Use a comma before a confirmatory question.

   a. It's a muggy day, isn't it?
   b. He has a delightfully dry sense of humour, hasn't he?
   c. She broke her glasses, didn't she?

14. Use a comma following the salutation (greeting) in a friendly letter.

   a. Dear Mother,
   b. Dear John,
   c. Andy,

15. Use commas in dates and addresses.
    NOTE:
    1. When the sentence continues following the year, the comma is required.
    2. Use a comma to separate the province from the postal code if they appear on the same line.

   a. On January 13, 1948, my brother was born in New Dominion, Prince Edward Island, during a snowstorm when my mother could not get to the Prince Edward Island Hospital in Charlottetown.
   b. Betty paid off her mortgage on April 29, 1994, on her 99 Ellerslie Avenue, Willowdale, Ontario, property.

16. Use commas to prevent misreading.

   a. Flipping the omelette over, Tony looked playfully at Mai.
   b. After eating, the children played in the yard.
   c. Without his wife, John would be "Ruth-less" and Ruth would be "Savage".

The Careful Eye

Semicolons

The semicolon is often used interchangeably with the period when two related sentences are to be connected. Secondly, it can replace both the comma and the conjunction in a compound sentence. Obviously, it cannot appear as terminal punctuation, but when used internally or when reading the sentence aloud, its function is closer to the period than it is to the comma. Note that the semicolon and the comma are not substitutes for each other.

1. Use a semicolon between independent clauses not joined by a co-ordinate conjunction. That is, a semicolon can be used to join two complete sentences that are related to each other.

   a. Harvard Graphics will be taught at Humber; anyone who wishes may join the class.
   b. The slogan "Reduce, Re-use, Recycle" has worked its way into the consciousness of a generation concerned about the environment; this generation now faithfully puts its bottles and cans into blue boxes and its coffee grounds and vegetable waste into backyard composters.
   c. Princess Diana has a right to privacy; the tabloids could leave her alone.
   d. Prince Charles has an outstanding knowledge of architecture; architecture and aesthetics must be complementary.

2. Conjunctive adverbs

are used for joining independent clauses. They are preceded by a semicolon and followed by a comma. Single syllable conjunctive adverbs (underscored in the following list) need no comma following them.

also	anyhow	as a result	besides
consequently	for example	furthermore	<u>hence</u>
however	in addition	in fact	instead
likewise,	meanwhile	moreover	namely
nevertheless	otherwise	similarly	<u>still</u>
<u>then</u>	therefore	<u>thus</u>	

   a. Harvard Graphics will be taught at Humber; however, only those who pay the fee will be enrolled in the class.
   b. Cities face a new problem because of the success of the blue box program; as a result, there is too much garbage and increasingly fewer municipalities who want to take it.
   c. The constitutional debate is nearly over; nevertheless, senate reform still needs resolution.

    d. Nearly all premiers agreed to meet for the discussions; still Quebec's premier refused to attend the sessions in Toronto.

3. **Use a semicolon to join independent clauses joined by a co-ordinate conjunction when there are already commas within either of the clauses. These sentences will be either compound or compound-complex**

    a. People will spend their money shopping, skiing, or vacationing; but they could also spend it on education, RRSPs, and taxes.
    b. Conduct, not sexuality, is the test for military or religious service; yet living honestly is preferable to living dishonourably.
    c. The Triple-E senate, supported by Manitoba, Saskatchewan, and Alberta, seems unlikely now; yet Joe Clark proposed a last-minute alternative.
    d. Today we can buy garden supplies from garden centres, lumber stores, and supermarkets; but a generation ago in the country, when such outlets did not exist, people relied on the corner store.

4. **Use a semicolon between items in a series when there are commas within the items of the series itself. These are simple sentences.**

    a. At the Acadia alumni dinner, I sat with the soon-to-be-former president, J. R. C. Perkin; the director of admissions, Robert Stead; and the past president, J. M. R. Beveridge.
    b. The Mexican travellers visited St. Boniface, Manitoba; Red Lake, Ontario; Moose Jaw, Saskatchewan, and Nanaimo, British Columbia.
    c. At our annual baseball game, I played on the team with Peter Coplestone, a consultant from Australia; Michael Wills, a consultant from Toronto; Jan Brewster, Susan Allan, and Ron and Sue Wakelin, teachers from southern Ontario; and Michael Wilson, a Toronto corporate real estate executive.
    d. Pamela Hanft, dean; Joe Aversa, chairman; Barbara Danbrook and Joan Pilz, co-ordinators; and Nancy Wade, organizational expert, attended the special meeting.

5. **Use a semicolon before an expression such as for example** (e.g.), **that is** (i.e.), **for instance, that is to say,** or **namely** when it is used to introduce a list of three or more items. Place a comma after such an expression.

    a. The dancer used terms not all students understood; that is to say, Russian bourée, plié, bourée derriere, Pas de Basques, High Cut and Travel, and entrechat.
    b. The artist's work sold especially well in three of the Atlantic provinces; namely, Prince Edward Island, Nova Scotia, and Newfoundland.

Colons

Colons are used in the following ways:

1. To introduce an explanation, example, or appositive
2. To introduce a series of three or more or a formal quotation
3. To separate hours and minutes and seconds and to form ratios
4. To separate biblical chapter numbers from verses
5. To separate titles and subtitles
6. To separate publication place from publishing company in bibliography
7. To follow salutations in business letters

---

1. The Toronto Maple Leafs are denied one thing: the Stanley Cup.

2. Pierre Trudeau had advice for everyone, especially journalists, who questioned his decisions: "Well, just watch me!"

3. When renovating a house, remember one thing: protect your investment in writing.

4. Successful bidders for the renovations will be evaluated by the following criteria:
   A. Cost
   B. Compatability and communication
   C. Qualifications and references

5. The first story of creation in The Holy Bible begins at Genesis 1:1 and ends at 2:2.

6. The shortest verse in the Holy Bible is St. John 11:35. It reads: "Jesus wept."

7. The telethon begins on Friday at 21:59:33.

8. Kathryn Schmidt's <u>The Home Remodeling Management Book: How to Plan, Organize and Manage Your Home Remodeling Project</u> is clearly illustrated.

9 Holmes. Donald E. <u>The Careful Eye: Proofreading and Editing Exercises</u>. Toronto: Thompson Educational Publishing, 1991.

10. The odds of winning the prize are 1000:1.

Dashes

1. Use a dash to set off parenthetical elements within a sentence. Material contained between dashes is **emphasized**.

   a. The Canadian Shield's raw materials – minerals- – cannot be easily extracted from the rock.
   b. Three experienced dancers – Carolyn MacMillan, Catherine Bell, Nora Fitzgerald – covered for the error of the novice dancer.

2. Use a dash to indicate interruption within a sentence.

   a. This book will be completed – regardless of bureaucratic restrictions – by the end of May!
   b. You should vote for the best candidate – no, you should vote for the only woman on the team.

3. Use a dash to set off a summarizing statement.

   a. Beginning with the left foot, walk in a straight line, first on the heel of the foot and then on the ball, and allow time to close your feet before the next move – these are the techniques for waltz.
   b. In a charity auction I am somewhat in their faces. I can be flippant. The point is to be amusing. It's not church; we're supposed to have fun, whereas an art auction has a degree of church – it is the holy grail of art.

4. Use a dash to attribute a quotation to an author.

   a. "Listening is a more complicated task in decision-making groups than in one-to-one communication." – Gerald L. Wilson.
   b. "Some acts of love are mere biology, some a sacrament." – Nancy Baker, The Night Shade.
   c. "Sic is Latin for **so** and is used to confirm the accuracy of the quotation. Yes, I do mean that in spite of your natural doubts. It should only be used when doubt is natural." – W. H. Fowler, A Dictionary of Modern English Usage.

The Careful Eye

Brackets

1. Use brackets to enclose **your own remarks** within a quotation; often the additional material is for the reader's clarification.

   a. A Texan hamburger weighs one kilogram [2.2 lbs.].
   b. There may be some programs in the next one [budget], but the MPs are not going on any large-scale spending spree.
   c. When two people marry, they sometimes experience term oil [sic] like fighting and conflict of interest.

   NOTE: In formal academic writing, <u>sic</u> means there is an error in the original and you choose to leave it as you find it.

Quotation Marks

1. Use quotation marks to enclose direct quotations.

   a. "Attention, energy, and commitment are the requirements for success," said Cecilia Grabbenclutch.
   b. "Your assignments will be due," said the professor, "at the beginning of the class."
   c. In a recent prison report, Millhaven authorities described Roch Thériault as "co-operative," adding that he seems "amenable to the rehabilitation process".

2. Use single quotation marks to enclose quotations within quotations.

   a. She said, "I'm sure I marked the package 'Fragile' before I mailed it".
   b. "There is nothing in the budget except the standard 'increased costs,'" said Mr. Moore.

3. Use quotation marks to enclose words used in a special sense.

   a. The package was marked "Fragile".
   b. The council decision was "off the wall".

4. Use a quotation mark to enclose a definition.

   a. In Early Childhood Education, "doing a creative" means "telling a story to children".
   b. Julius Caesar's statement, "Omnia Gallia in tres partes divisa est" means "all Gaul was divided into three parts".

5. Use quotation marks to enclose titles of literary works such as magazine and newspaper articles, chapters of books, poems, lectures, and songs. The titles of magazines, newspapers, books, long poems, albums, and CDs are italicized or underlined where italics are not possible.

   a. Craig Barrett wrote "Effective Note-Taking" in <u>The Anti-Flunk Book</u>.
   b. "Edith Awarded Inheritance," airing originally in 1979 on <u>All In the Family</u>, starred Jean Stapleton as Edith and Carroll O'Connor as Archie.

Parentheses

Use parentheses to set off nonessential sentence elements; in fact, anything in parentheses within a sentence is **deemphasized**.

   a. These three products (mangos, passion fruit, and avocados) come from Chile.
   b. The last instruction (in Appendix D) is redundant.
   c. A brilliant student at convent school and at the University of Ottawa, Jeanne Mathilde Benoit (Mathilde was the midwife's name at her birth) became active at 15 in a reformist Catholic students' movement, Jeunesse étudiante catholique.

The Careful Eye

Italics

Use **italics** to indicate words that would be italicized if they were included in print. Italics are normally used for titles of books, magazines, newspapers, complete works published separately, including long poems and works of art.

*NOTE: When italics cannot be reproduced on the typewriter or computer, **underlining is the standard substitution**.*

a. Groups in Context is published by McGraw-Hill.
b. Brian Segal is the publisher of Maclean's, Canada's weekly magazine.
c. Prince Edward Island's main newspapers, The Guardian and The Evening Patriot, cover the Island like the dew.
d. John Milton wrote Paradise Lost, and he was imprisoned for his writing of this work.
e. Tom Thomson, who was an acquaintance of but who was not a member of the Canadian Group of Seven, painted The Frozen Lake.

Hyphens

1. Hyphenate compound adjectives preceding nouns, but not following them. The exceptions to this rule are some permanently hyphenated words like **out-of-date, first-class, full-time, up-to-date, old-fashioned, short-term, well-known, and well-rounded**.

   a. tough-minded executive
   b. executive who is tough minded
   c. brown-skinned man
   d. man who is brown skinned
   e. all-you-can-eat buffet
   f. buffet offering all you can eat

2. Hyphenate prefixes.
   *NOTE: Prefixes **dis**, **pre**, **non**, and **un** generally require no hyphen even if the last letter of the prefix is repeated as in the following words: dissimilar, preemergent, nonnutritive, and unnatural.*

   a. post-war trauma
   b. ex-lover
   c. anti-feminism

3. Hyphenate to avoid confusion with homonyms. Notice the differences in both the pronunciation and the meaning of the paired words.

   a. re-cover and recover
   b. re-creation and recreation
   c. re-lease and release
   d. re-lent and relent
   e. re-present and represent
   f. re-press and repress
   g. re-sign and resign
   h. re-sort and resort

4. Hyphenate suspended compound adjectives where the noun is used only once.

   a. In college, we teach eighteen-, nineteen-, and twenty-year-olds.
   b. The students applied for both part- and full-time jobs.

The Careful Eye

> 5. Hyphenate fractions and compound numbers.

a. Three-fifths of the students are prepared for the exam.
b. The most useful wrench is a nine-sixteenths.
c. Seventy-five per cent of the funds went to a children's charity.

> 6. In bibliography, use **three** hyphens to cite the second and subsequent entries by the same author. In short, three hyphens and a period replace the author's name. If you can key an M–rule on your typewriter or word processor, you may use it in place of three hyphens.

Montgomery, Lucy Maud. <u>Akin to Anne: Tales of Other Orphans</u>. Rea Wilmshurst, ed. Toronto: McClelland and Stewart, 1989.
—. <u>Anne of Ingleside</u>. Toronto: McClelland-Bantam, Inc., 1983.
—. <u>Pat of Silver Bush</u>. Toronto: McClelland and Stewart Limited, 1989.

The Careful Eye

Apostrophes

1. Use apostrophes to indicate the **possessive** form of nouns. Singular possession is formed by adding **'s** to the singular noun.

   a. The girl's shoes are Reeboks.
   b. When did Tom tune Charlie's piano?
   c. The child's games seem complicated.
   d. Today's plan is clear.
   e. The man's name is Neil, but his son's name is Noel.
   f. The woman's job is top secret.
   g. My boss's friend is Francine.
      Note: The 's is traditional; The modern method is to drop the final s
   h. Bryden's teeth are his dentist's pride.
   i. My mother's name is Burdena, and her sister's name is Jemima.
   j. Sophie's Choice is a serious movie.
   k. That man's and woman's wedding bands are wide!
   l. The nation's business seems important to its people.
   m. The dancer's pride is in performing well; the gambler's, in winnings.
   n. Toronto's garbage could have been handled in Kirkland Lake's mines.

2. Plural possession is formed by adding **'s** to the plural noun.

   Alternative method to create plural possession:
   a. Change a singular noun to plural: **chair** becomes **chairs**.
   b. Add an **'s** to the plural noun: **chairs** becomes **chairs's**.
   c. Check for double or triple **s** sound; it is double in **chairs's**.
   d. If a double or triple **s** sound exists, **drop the final s**, leaving the apostrophe in place: **chairs'**.

   a. The girls' shoes are Nikes.
   b. The children's games seem complicated.
   c. Five days' work is sufficient.
   d. The men's names are Nathan and Gursev.
   e. The women's jobs are confidential.
   f. My bosses' names are Francine and Francis.
   g. My grandfathers' ancestry is British.
   h. Many Canadian citizens' backgrounds are diverse.
   i. The flowers' scent is sweet.
   j. The books' titles are The Gage Canadian Dictionary and The Oxford English Dictionary.

49

The Careful Eye

Study these examples:

Singular	Plural	Possessive	Revision
box	boxes	boxes's	boxes'
man	men	men's	men's
woman	women	women's	women's
child	children	children's	children's
book	books	books's	books'
movie	movies	movies's	movies'
jackpot	jackpots	jackpots's	jackpots'
astronaut	astronauts	astronauts's	astronauts'

> 3. Use the apostrophe to show **omission** of one or more letters in contractions. The application of this rule applies to informal writing, but not to business or formal writing where abbreviations are discouraged.

Contraction	Full form
it's	**it is**
isn't	is not
hasn't	has not
haven't	have not
aren't	are not
she's	she is
he's	he is
they're	**they are**
we're	**we are**
you're	you are
who's	who is
we've	we have
he'll	he will
you'll	you will
shouldn't	should not
wouldn't	would not
couldn't	could not
can't	can not
won't	will not
o'clock	of the clock
'tis	it is
doesn't	does not
don't	do not

The Careful Eye

> 4. Use the apostrophe to form the plural of symbols, letters, figures, and words used as words.
> *NOTE: When any of this group is italicized, the 's for the plural is not italicized.*

a. Indent all ¶'s in semiblock letters.
b. All uses of £'s are likely British.
c. He wrote peculiar D's.
d. Accommodate has two a's, two c's, two m's, and two o's.
e. Your 7's look like 2's.
f. Use fewer and's and but's in your writing.

NOTE: Common practise now is to omit the apostrophe with the symbols, figures, and dates. The apostrophe is retained only for letters that would make complete words and therefore cause confusion upon reading: **Is and as are both vowels.** *In that example, confusion results, so the apostrophe is used:* **I's and a's are both vowels.**

> 5. If an apostrophe is used to show the plural, another apostrophe may be deleted in the same word to show omission.

the 60's   the 70's   the 90's

> 6. Use an apostrophe to show plural or joint possession, and to do so, add the apostrophe only to the second noun.

1. Tom and Betty's parties are lively.
2. Bupinder and Shandi's kirpans are antiques.
3. Debbie and Wayne's daughter is tall for her age.
4. Brad and Betty's tango is sensual.
5. Kelly and Leigh's signatures are identical.

> 7. Avoid apostrophes with possessive personal pronouns. **my, mine, your, yours, his, her, hers, its, our, ours, their, theirs**

1. His and her signatures are similar.
2. This computer is mine; that one is theirs.
3. The design of your house is pleasing; its proportion is better than ours.
4. The B&G is mine, not theirs; the Bristol Cream must be yours or hers.

Its, It's, . . . and Its'

The frequency with which the possessive pronoun **its** and its companion **it's**, the contracted form of **it is**, are confused is prolific. A contraction means that one or more letters are dropped from a word, and the apostrophe is used to replace the omitted letter or letters. For instance, **does not** becomes **doesn't**, and **of the clock** becomes **o'clock**. When the words **it** and **is** form one short, single-syllable word, we omit the **i** from the word **is**; then we replace that **i** with an apostrophe. The result is the single word **it's**, but the new word **it's** retains the same meaning as the original words from which it came. There is no change in meaning.

Notice what happens in the following sentences:
1. **I see a cardinal flying to her nest.**

Now look at the following sentence still about the cardinal flying to the same nest.
2. **It is** flying to her nest.

This sentence could also be written as:
3. **It's** flying to her nest.

In that statement, the only change has been in the deletion of **i** from the word **is**.

Let's effect a second change still about the cardinal going to the same nest, but this time using **it's** and **its** together.
4. **It's** flying to **its** nest.

The foregoing sentence, if it were read in full, would read:
5. **It is** flying to **its** nest.

We know that the first word of the sentence is correct--we've already agreed to it, but if we were to read "**It is** flying to **it is** nest," we immediately hear that the latter sentence makes no sense in English.

Therefore, if we substitute **it is** for **its** and the meaning is nonsense, we can be sure that **it's** is the **wrong** word to use in that case. Every time we write **it's**, we must be able to read what we have written as **it is** in the sentence, and that sentence must make sense. Finally, the correct choice, then, at the end of sentence five is **its**.

Whenever we use **it's** in a sentence, we are using a subject (it) and a verb (is). We are then making a statement of fact. Whenever we use **its**, we are using a possessive pronoun. Note that this word is already possessive and **does not require an apostrophe** to make it "more" possessive. The possessive pronoun **its** is often followed by a noun: **its** wing, **its** tail, **its** flight, **its** colour.

Examine the following examples using **it's**

It's summer.
It's raining.
It's recycled paper.
It's easy to follow.
It's noon.

In the above cases where we've used **it's** we could substitute **it is** and each substitution would make sense.

It's summer means the same as **it is** summer.
It's raining means the same as **it is** raining.
It's recycled paper means the same as **it is** recycled paper.
It's easy to follow means the same as **it is** easy to follow.
It's noon means the same as **it is** noon.

Here are four additional examples where only **it's** can be used:

1. <u>Me: Stories of My Life</u> is about Katharine Hepburn; **it's** her autobiography.
2. This book is a confessional and a journal; **it's** immediate!
3. But **it's** fabulous reading material because her voice comes through in every line.
4. True to her form, Hepburn leaves her audience wanting more; **it's** not a full revelation of her love affair with Spencer Tracy.

The Careful Eye

Exercises using It's, Its, and Its'

> If the two words **it is** make sense when reading the sentence, then use either **it is** or **it's**. If **it is** does not make sense in the sentence, then use the possessive pronoun **its**.

1. **(It's, Its)** easy learning contractions!
2. **(It's, Its)** difficult to ski on one foot.
3. **(It's, Its)** natural to be happy.
4. **(It's, Its)** necessary that we eat healthful food.
5. **(It's, Its)** my job, and **(it's, its)** fun to do it well.
6. **(It's, Its)** time to go to college, said he.
7. **(It's, Its)** not, said she.
8. **(It's, Its)** true, thought she.
9. Where is my grammar book? **(It's, Its)** filed on the floor.
10. **(It's, Its)** in **(it's, its)** normal place, responded she.
11. **(It's, Its)** place is not the floor; **(it's, its)** the shelf.
12. But **(it's, its)** not in **(it's, its)** place on **(it's, its)** shelf.
13. Where could it be? **(It's, Its)** in my briefcase.
14. **(It's, Its)** time to end this exercise, since **(it's, its)** the first time I have answered all questions correctly.

> Some people attempt to use **its'** as the plural form of **its**. **There is no such word in the English language as its'!** The plural of **its** is **their**, and neither one uses an apostrophe to show possession.

15. **(It's, Its, Its')** incorrect to use **(it's, its, its')**.
16. That door has three hinges; **(it's, its, its')** hinges are brass.
17. Of the three words--it's, its, its'-- only **(it's, its, its')** is always incorrect.
18. Of the three words--it's, its, and its'--it is never correct to use **it's, its, its'** when you write.
19. **(It's, Its, Its')** is a possessive pronoun, third person singular.
20. The contraction of **it is** must always be written as **(it's, its)**.

Sentence Patterns

Clauses

I. **Simple Sentences**
express one complete idea in one independent clause.

II. **Compound Sentences**
express two or more main ideas in two or more independent clauses.

III. **Complex Sentences**
contain one independent or main clause and one or more dependent or subordinate clauses

IV. **Compound-compex Sentences**
contain two or more dependent clauses and at least one independent clause

Phrases

I. **Prepositional**

II. **Participal**

III. **Gerund**

IV. **Infinitive**

The Careful Eye

Simple Sentences

> **Simple sentences** express one idea; that is, they contain only one independent or main clause. Each of the following sentences has one main subject and one main verb or compounds of these elements that still produce one main idea. Study the variety that exists within these simple sentences. In each sentence, underline the subject once and the verb twice.

Exercises

1. A lynx weighs up to 18 kilograms. (subject and verb)

2. The lynx is stealthy.
   (subject, linking verb, adjective complement)

3. Wolves, cougars, and humans prey upon lynx.
   (compound subject and verb)

4. Lynx search for the carcasses of moose and caribou and eat hare and birds.
   (subject and compound verb)

5. The lynx, one of British Columbia's three wildcats, is a stealthy animal, stalking its victims at night, biding by day in coniferous forests.
   (subject and verb separated by prepositional phrases, participles)

6. These long-legged cats, weighing up to 18 kilograms, are most common in northern British Columbia.
   (subject and verb separated by participle)

7. Like its cousins, the bobcat and the cougar, the lynx hunts by sight, leaping great distances to pounce on its prey.
   (introductory phrases preceding subject and verb, participle)

8. Like its cousins, the bobcat and the cougar, the lynx hunts by sight and leaps great distances to pounce on its prey.
   (introductory phrases, subject and compound verb)

9. The cougar and lynx hunt and stalk their prey.
   (compound subject and compound verb)

10. Fitz Hugh Sound, British Columbia, is a reliable humpback sight in autumn. (subject and verb)

11. Within the first three decades of this century, more than 23,000 humpbacks, including nearly 3,000 off British Columbia's coast, were slaughtered in the North Pacific.
    (two introductory prepositional phrases, subject, participle, verb)

12. Grey whales feed on herring spawn in Clayoquot Sound.
    (subject, verb, two prepositional phrases)

13. Study in the morning.
    (subject implied, verb, prepositional phrase)

14. Pray.
    (subject implied, verb)

15. According to a leading expert, a Mercedes could outlast the world!
    (introductory prepositional phrase, subject, verb)

16. For greater strength, Mercedes uses more welds than most other car makers.
    (introductory prepositional phrase, subject, verb)

17. In fact, the body of a Mercedes-Benz is welded together at up to 5,000 points, with some as little as 20 millimetres apart.
    (subject, prepositional phrase, verb)

18. Don't you believe it?
    (verb separated by subject)

19. For a large colour portfolio featuring classic rattan furniture and seven special collections, send $25.00 to Box 763, Station A, Toronto, Ontario.
    (introductory prepositional phrase, implied subject, verb)

20. Try to study regularly.
    (implied subject, verb)

21. Practise, James, for your evening performance.
    (verb, subject)

22. Practise scrabble for your own benefit in the game.
    (implied subject, verb, prepositional phrases)

The Careful Eye

Answers – Simple Sentences

SUBJECT	VERB
1. lynx	1. weighs
2. lynx	2. is
3. Wolves, cougars, humans	3. prey
4. lynx	4. search / eat
5. lynx	5. is
6. cats	6. are
7. lynx	7. hunts
8. lynx	8. hunts / leaps
9. cougar / lynx	9. hunt / stalk
10. Fitz Hugh Sound	10. is
11. humpbacks	11. were slaughtered
12. whales	12. feed
13. (You)	13. Study
14. (You)	14. Pray
15. Mercedes	15. could outlast
16. Mercedes	16. uses
17. body	17. is welded
18. You	18. do believe
19. (You)	19. send
20. (You)	20. try
21. James	21. Practise
22. (You)	22. Practise

Compound Sentences

Compound sentences express a minimum of two main ideas; however, there may be more than two main ideas. Each idea in a compound sentence contains both a subject and a verb and stands independently. To join the ideas in a compound sentence, the following methods of punctuation are standard:

1. Use a comma followed by a co-ordinating conjunction
2. Use a semicolon
3. Use a semicolon followed by a conjunctive adverb and a comma

In the following sentences, underline the subjects of each sentence once and the verbs of the sentences twice. Finally, observe the standard punctuation used here to join the ideas.

NOTE: in compound sentences, there will be a minimum of two subjects and two verbs for each sentence.

Exercises

1. Lynx search for the carcasses of moose and caribou, and they also eat hare and birds.
   (subject, verb, comma and conjunction, subject, verb)

2. The bobcat and cougar are cousins of the lynx; they too hunt by sight and pounce upon their prey.
   (compound subject and single verb, semicolon, single subject and compound verb)

3. The bobcat and the cougar are cousins of the lynx; they hunt by sight, and they pounce upon their prey.
   (compound subject and single verb, semicolon, subject and verb, subject and verb)

4. Bobcats hunt their prey, yet lynx stalk it.
   (subject and verb, subject and verb)

5. The lynx is not an endangered species, yet in 1989, 8,265 Canadian lynx pelts fetched nearly $2 million.
   (subject and verb, conjunction, subject and verb)

6. Women are not chattels; they are intelligent and human.
   (subject and verb, semicolon, subject and verb)

The Careful Eye

7. Doug Gilmour is the Leafs' most valuable player; therefore, he is expected to receive the Hart trophy in 1993.
(subject and verb, semicolon and conjunctive adverb and comma, and subject and verb)

8. Teemu Selanne will likely win the Calder trophy for Rookie of the Year; he has already scored 76 goals with the Winnipeg Jets.
(subject and verb, semicolon, subject and verb)

9. Mario Lemieux won the Art Ross trophy for leading scorer, yet he succeeded despite battling Hodgkin's disease, a form of lymphatic cancer.
(subject and verb, comma and co-ordinating conjunction, subject and verb)

10. The Great One, Wayne Gretzky, has realized another "first"; in 1993, he was overlooked as an award finalist.
(subject and verb, semicolon, subject and verb)

The Careful Eye

Answers

SUBJECT	VERB
1. Lynx they	2. search eat
2. bobcat / cougar they	2. are hunt / pounce
3. bobcat / cougar they they	3. are hunt pounce
4. Bobcats lynx	4. hunt stalk
5. lynx pelts	5. is fetched
6. Women they	6. are are
7. Doug Gilmour he	7. is is
8. Teemu Selanne he	8. will win has scored
9. Mario Lemieux he	9. won succeeded
10. The Great One he	10. has realized was overlooked

The Careful Eye

Complex Sentences

Complex sentences contain one main or independent clause **and** one or more subordinate clauses. The dependent clause begins with a subordinating conjunction which will prevent that idea from existing as a complete thought. Dependent ideas or clauses contain a subject and a verb, but they cannot stand independently. Dependent ideas are <u>usually</u> joined to independent ones by a comma. Independent clauses can be placed at the beginning, middle, or end of a sentence.

Identify the subjects and the verbs in these complex sentences; be careful to select only the subjects and verbs from the <u>independent</u> clauses.

Exercises

1. While the lynx is an expert tree climber and powerful swimmer, it can run silently and quickly over soft snow because of its big furry feet.
   (dependent clause, subject and verb, dependent clause)

2. Because the lynx rests during the day, it catches its prey during the night.
   (dependent clause, subject and verb)

3. The lynx (<u>Lynx</u> <u>canadensis</u>) lives primarily in northern British Columbia since an abundance of its prey, the snowshoe hare, thrives there.
   (subject and verb, dependent clause)

4. A Grey whale's eyeball, which is located at the binge of its jaw, is difficult to detect at first glance with the naked eye.
   (subject, dependent clause, verb)

5. According to their data, nearly 98 percent of all Mercedes that have been registered in the last fifteen years are still on the road.
   (prepositional phrase, subject, prepositional phrase, dependent clause, verb)

6. It's no wonder you often see old Mercedes driving around with hundreds of thousands of miles on them.
   (subject and verb, dependent clause)

7. As you see, while other car makers build their cars to last for years, Mercedes-Benz has built a reputation for cars that last for decades.
   (two dependent clauses, subject and verb, dependent clause)

8. Dave Andreychuk, who is a go-to-the-net kind of player, tied Lanny McDonald's record of ten goals in one playoff season.
   (subject, dependent clause, verb)

9. Silken Lauman deserved much more than a bronze olympic medal because she fought incredible personal odds.
   (subject and verb, dependent clause)

10. The Quebec government demanded that every worker make concessions now to help alleviate the financial crisis.
    (subject and verb, dependent clause)

11. Award the Boris-Brian boar pelt to whoever killed it.
    (implied subject, verb, dependent clause)

12. Patients who exhibit "white coat syndrome" rarely need hypertension medication.
    (subject, dependent clause, verb)

13. Five million Canadians or more take drugs that treat a disease they may not even have.
    (subject and verb, two dependent clauses)

14. June Rowlands was the mayor who wanted department heads, not City of Toronto councillors, on the Toronto Harbour Commission.
    (subject and verb, dependent clause)

15. Joe Clark, who worked tirelessly on the Canadian constitution, may enter the Conservative leadership race, which ends with a leadership convention June 13.
    (subject, dependent clause, verb, dependent clause)

16. New Democrat MP Steven Langdon, who delivered a scathing public attack on Bob Rae's deficit-fighting strategy, criticized the Premier because of controversial budget cuts and tax hikes.
    (subject, dependent clause, verb, dependent clause)

17. Miriam Bedard, who won two gold medals in the 1994 Winter Olympics in Lillihammer, Norway, deserved to be named Canada's woman athlete of the year.

The Careful Eye

Answers – Complex Sentences

SUBJECT	VERB
1. it	2. can run
2. it	2. catches
3. lynx	3. lives
4. eyeball	4. is
5. percent	5. are
6. It	6. is
7. Mercedes-Benz	7. has built
8. Dave Andreychuk	8. tied
9. Silken Lauman	9. deserved
10. government	10. demanded
11. (You)	11. Award
12. Patients	12. need
13. more	13. take
14. June Rowlands	14. was
15. Joe Clark	15. may enter
16. Steven Langdon	16. criticized
17. Miriam Bedard	17. deserved

Compound-Complex Sentences

> Compound-complex sentences contain two or more independent clauses and at least one dependent clause. The placement of the dependent clauses can be at the beginning, at the end, or in the middle of the sentence. As in complex sentences, the main subjects and verbs are found only in the **independent** clauses. Study the variety that exists within these sentences, noting particularly the placement of the dependent clauses. For each of these compound-complex sentences, identify the subject and the verb working only from the independent clauses.

Exercises

1. The lynx normally bears two or three kittens annually, yet, when the food supply is abundant, she can bear as many as six kittens in one litter.
   (independent clause, dependent clause, independent clause)

2. Fitz Hugh Sound, which is over 100 kilometres northeast of Vancouver Island, and which is a prime viewing area of humpback whales, allows scientists to distinguish one whale from another; they photograph scratches, nicks, and other permanent marks on each whale.
   (independent clause interrupted by two dependent clauses; independent clause)

3. Do women feel that they must emulate a model, or do they feel that self-satisfaction is the measure of maturity?
   (independent clause, dependent clause; independent clause, dependent clause)

4. Many Croats, who are trying to push Muslims across the Neretva River, want to unite southwestern Bosnia with neighbouring Croatia; similarly, Serbs desire linking areas they control in Croatia with Serbia.
   (independent clause interrupted by dependent clause; independent clause, dependent clause)

5. Because the spike is designed to damage logging equipment that comes in contact with it, logging operators claim that it has the potential to injure workers; consequently, even "innocent" acts of vandalism threaten the giant Sitka spruce of the Clayoquot rain forest in British Columbia.
   (dependent clause, independent clause, dependent clause; independent clause)

The Careful Eye

6. Over 83,000 Canadian children, 11 to 14 years of age, who grew up in a drug generation, used steroids to help them look better; some of them used drugs to improve athletic performance.

7. Keeping jobs in small towns in Quebec is difficult; the growing militancy, which has become a trend, stresses the need for economic help in rural Quebec.

8. A mysterious illness, which started in New Mexico and which has flu-like symptoms, has health officials worried; it is a virus which struck native Americans as well as those non-natives attending them.

9. McDonald's is convenient; although it is relatively inexpensive, it serves hamburgers without fillers.

10. Because it is a matter of life or death, mercy killing's morality split 1500 Alberta doctors; medication can keep all but a very few "comfortable" until natural death.

11. While in the Yukon, Louis wanted to be successful; he wanted to find a narwal tusk.

12. Ross, who is an archaeologist, found diamonds; he was seeking fossils.

13. If your stomach is upset, trust Maalox; it is guaranteed to work.

14. If you insist, lie; I don't advise it.

15. When you are tired, rest; it helps.

Answers – Compound-Complex Sentences

SUBJECT	VERB
1. lynx she	1. bears can bear
2. Fitz Hugh Sound they	2. allows photograph
3. women they	3. do feel do feel
4. Croats Serbs	4. want desire
5. operators acts	5. claim threaten
6. children some	6. used used
7. Keeping jobs in small towns militancy	7. is stresses
8. illness it	8. has is
9. McDonald's it	9. is serves
10. morality medication	10. split can keep
11. Louis he	11. wanted wanted
12. Ross he	12. found was seeking
13. (You) it	13. trust is
14. (You) I	14. lie do advise
15. (You) it	15. rest helps

The Careful Eye

Phrases

1. **Prepositional phrases** begin with a preposition and end with a noun.

    a. **beside** the planter
    b. **of** the roadside screening devices
    c. **on account of** his condition
    d. **notwithstanding** the complaint
    e. **with respect to** your request
    f. **without** exception

2. **Participial phrases** include a participle and its modifiers. Participial phrases **always** function as adjectives.

    a. **Using the Draegar ALCOTEST 7410 machine to replace the ALERT device**, the O.P.P. have reinstated the spot test for drinking and driving.
    b. The morning of May 21, 1993, **darkened by a partial eclipse**, reached a record low temperature.
    c. **Being deluded about the requirements for getting a job**, the teenager dropped out of highschool.
    d. **Charmed by adventure**, they travelled to Europe and Africa.

3. **Gerund phrases** contain a gerund and one or more modifiers; these phrases function as **nouns**.

    a. They won the contest **learning how to dance**.
    b. Bertha's ultimate goal was **being healthy and happy and old**.
    c. **Complaining without working** invites disapproval.
    d. **Driving a motorcycle** requires skill.
    e. **Memorizing the times tables** and **reading with comprehension** are basic skills students need in college and in the workforce.

4. **Infinitive phrases** contain an infinitive and can be used as a noun or its modifier.

    a. The Miss Saigon cast plans **to rehearse diligently** for its opening on May 26.
    b. The political neophyte chose **to exercise power rather than reason**.
    c. **To consider others** demonstrates maturity.
    d. Flexibility is **to dance a calypso rhythm**.

68

5. **Absolute phrases** consist of a noun followed and modified by a participle or participial phrase. An absolute phrase or clause modifies **no** single word in a sentence, yet it is related to the sentence.

   a. **Dusk approaching**, the cardinals fed their young.
   b. **A thunderstorm threatening**, we swam to shore.
   c. **The series ended**, <u>Cheers'</u> fans gathered in SkyDome for the final episode.
   d. **Hailing the Leafs**, we celebrated their return.
   e. They entered the trust company, **indifference coming from within.**

Section II: Exercises With Answers

The Careful Eye

Agreement

A singular subject takes a singular verb; a plural subject, a plural verb.

1. The data (is, are) correct.
2. The girls in the choir (sing, sings) well.
3. One of the reasons (was, were) that she was tired.
4. All people (is, are) equal.
5. His trousers (seem, seems) too short.
6. The evening news (tell, tells) of the day's events.
7. Politics (is, are) an interesting career.
8. The scissors (is, are) in the cabinet.

Indefinite pronouns take singular verbs.

9. Each of the girls (give, gives) her help.
10. Neither of the answers (is, are) correct.
11. Everyone (like, likes) the movie.
12. Either of them (is, are) going to help.
13. Everybody (has, have) (his or her, his, their) own ideas.
14. Each night somebody in the audience (laugh, laughs).

Collective nouns *usually* take singular verbs. However, when each person in the group acts separately of if there is disagreement or disunity in the actions of the group, then a plural verb is used.

15. The herd (is, are) grazing in the field.
16. The audience (is, are) arguing about the play's quality.
17. The class (go, goes) to the museum every Saturday.
18. The jury (deliberate, deliberates) in the jury room.

Part-Portion Rule

Words such as "some," "all," and fractions are neither singular nor plural on their own. Look at the complete subject in these cases; that is, include the prepositional phrase to make the object in the phrase agree with the verb.

19. Some of the cake (is, are) gone.
20. Some of the cakes (is, are) gone.
21. One-half of the girls (is, are) ready.
22. All of the children (play, plays).
23. Some of the money (was, were) lost.

The number is singular. A number is plural.

24. A number of people (is, are) interesting.
25. The number of applicants (is, are) increasing.
26. A number of reasons (was, were) given.
27. The great number of suggestions (call, calls) for discussion.

Sums of money and measurements are generally considered as a unit and therefore take a singular verb.

28. Nine weeks (is, are) a long holiday.
29. (Are, Is) $500 enough for our trip to Etobicoke?
30. Fifty miles (is, are) a long way to walk.

Compounds joined by "and" take a plural verb except when the two units are considered as one (Spaghetti and meatballs is a good dinner.) or when the subject is preceded by "each," "every," or "many a".

31. Mary and her sister (go, goes) swimming daily.
32. Each student and teacher (is, are) responsible for (his or her, their) own work.
33. Many a man and woman (fear, fears) the first day on a new job.
34. A block and tackle (is, are) used in construction.
35. Many men and women (wish, wishes) for success.
36. Peanut butter and jelly (is, are) my favourite sandwich.
37. Every man and woman in the department (is, are) qualified for the job.

When compounds are joined by "or" or "nor," the verb is determined by the nearer subject.

38. Neither the teacher nor the students (want, wants) to attend.
39. Neither the students nor the teacher (want, wants) to attend.
40. Either the children or their mother (is, are) mistaken about what happened.
41. Neither Josephine nor I (is, am, are) going to the market.

The Careful Eye

Relative pronouns
(who, which, that, whose, whom, whoever, whomever, whichever, whatever) are singular or plural depending on the word to which they refer. Generally, they refer to the word directly before them.
Exception: With the word "only": He is only one of the men who is helpful. Here "only" refers to one and the verb is therefore singular.

42. Each of us who (is, are) able should help.
43. He is one of the people who always (think, thinks) clearly.
44. She is the woman who (seem, seems) best qualified.
45. Emily is one of the girls who (travel, travels) annually.
46. Emily is only one of the girls who (travel, travels) daily.

Words joined to a subject by "with," "together with," "in addition to." "as well as," and "including" do not affect the verb choice. The verb will still agree with the subject preceding these words.

47. Our allies, as well as the enemy, (was, were) suffering.
48. My whole equipment, including fishing rods, tackle, and knapsack, (was, were) lost on the trip.

Forms of the verb to be agree with the subject, not with the complements (predicate noun or pronoun).

49. The hardest part of the job (is, are) the bending and lifting.
50. Bending and lifting (is, are) the hardest part of the job.

Answers:

1. are; 2. sing; 3. was; 4. are; 5. seem; 6. tells; 7. is; 8. are 9. gives; 10. is; 11. likes; 12. is; 13. has/his or her; 14. laughs; 15. is; 16. are; 17. goes; 18. deliberate 19. is; 20. are; 21. are; 22. play; 23. was; 24. are; 25. is; 26. were; 27. calls; 28. is; 29. Is; 30. is; 31. go; 32. is; 33. fears; 34. is; 35. wish; 36. is; 37. is; 38. want; 39. wants; 40. is; 41. am; 42. are; 43. think; 44. seems; 45. travel; 46. travels; 47. were; 48. was; 49. is; 50. are.

The Careful Eye

Comma Splices

Identify each numbered group of words as a sentence or as a comma splice. If it is a sentence, eliminate any unnecessary commas; if the punctuation is correct, leave it, and place C at the end of the sentence.

1. Rita decided to stop smoking, not wanting to die of lung cancer.
2. Mary was too ill to get up, she stayed in bed for the day.
3. Fred phoned his supervisor at his new job the night before he was going to start, just to make sure when he was supposed to be there.
4. The subway train rushed through the station, a blur of rush-hour passengers flashing in front of my eyes.
5. Jenny panicked, the car had stalled on a busy section of the highway.
6. The wedding reception began to get out of hand, after the bride's brother showed up with several of his noisy friends.
7. Larry's pitchfork turned over topsoil, earthworms poked their heads out of the cool spring soil.
8. Hundreds of crushed cars were piled in neat stacks, the rusted hulks like huge flattened tin cans.
9. The teacher was pleased with the class, they had done very well on their projects.
10. The class is going to be dismissed early, because no-one seems to have any questions about the work.
11. Something was wrong with the meatloaf, it had a strange taste to it.
12. The principal dismissed the school early on the day of the big snow storm, realizing that many students would have hours of bus travel before reaching home that night.
13. Adalja began screaming, her toothache was intolerable.
14. Brett moved from Brandon to Halifax, which was as far as he could get from his ex-girlfriend.
15. Huguette never eats breakfast, she's just not hungry in the mornings, especially at that time of day!

Answers
Abbreviations: C (correct sentence) cs (comma splice)

1. C	2. cs *up;*	3. C
4. C	5. cs *punished;*	6. C
7. cs *topsoil;*	8. C	9. cs *class;*
10. C (optional to delete comma)		11. cs *meatloaf;*
12. C		13. cs *screaming;*
14. C		15. cs *breakfast;*

The Careful Eye

Comma Splices, Run-ons

> Eliminate the comma splices and run-ons in the following article. Correct them by using a combination of punctuation and conjunctions where necessary, but avoid deleting or adding any other words.

Career Foundations

To be successful in a career, one must prepare adequately in college, work hard on the job, and communicate well with employers, colleagues, and the public. Career success, curiously enough, can be compared to the construction of a building.

When constructing anything, a strong foundation is a necessity, working hard in college lays the foundation for a successful career. By doing well in school, an individual receives not only a solid education but also direction in life and knowledge, careers also depend greatly upon how well one performs in his/her studies.

Working hard in a particular field is similar to giving a house the proper support beams to keep it standing. The stronger something is when it is erected, the more difficult it will be to bring down by working hard on the job, a person is laying the support beams for a strong and prosperous career. In keeping an employer happy, one's rewards can be plentiful. Hard work shows that a person cares about what is done and, if there is a caring attitude, there will always be a job suited to one's needs.

A finished product is a work of pride if it has been done properly, it can be something beautiful. Communicating well is also a finished product, it is polished, pleasing to the eye, and grabs one's attention. In the case of a finished house, people want to see it, just as in the case of people with good communication skills, others will come back to see them. It is something regrettable now, few people can communicate well.

Many similarities arise between a finished house and a strong career: good strong foundations are needed in both, there must be sturdy supports, and, in the end, there will always be beautifully finished products, it is important to remember that a successful career begins with a sound foundation.

The Careful Eye

Answers – Comma Splices, Run-ons
Underlining indicates where changes have been made.

To be successful in a career, one must prepare adequately in college, work hard on the job, and communicate well with employers, colleagues, and the public. Career success, curiously enough, can be compared to the construction of a building.

When constructing anything, a strong foundation is a necessity, so working hard in college lays the foundation for a successful career. By doing well in school, an individual receives not only a solid education but also direction in life and knowledge; careers also depend greatly upon how well one performs in his/her studies.

Working hard in a particular field is similar to giving a house the proper support beams to keep it standing. The stronger something is when it is erected, the more difficult it will be to bring down. By working hard on the job, a person is laying the support beams for a strong and prosperous career. In keeping an employer happy, one's rewards can be plentiful. Hard work shows that a person cares about what is done; and, if there is a caring attitude, there will always be a job suited to one's needs.

A finished product is a work of pride. If it has been done properly, it can be something beautiful. Communicating well is also a finished product; it is polished, pleasing to the eye, and grabs one's attention. In the case of a finished house, people want to see it; just as in the case of people with good communication skills, others will come back to see them. It is something regrettable now. Few people can communicate well.

Many similarities arise between a finished house and a strong career: good strong foundations are needed in both; there must be sturdy supports; and, in the end, there will always be beautifully finished products. It is important to remember that a successful career begins with a sound foundation.

Compound Sentences

> Revise the errors in the following sentences to make them accurate compound sentences. Use punctuation and additional words economically as required.

1. Sue Rodrigues wants to die with dignity and her case is before the Supreme court of Canada.

2. Mrs. Rodrigues would control the dying process and activate any device.

3. She is waiting for a judgement, and an approval.

4. Suicide is not illegal in Canada but helping someone to end her life is.

5. The moral and social issues make sense, the legalities do puzzle me.

6. Denying Mrs. Rodrigues control over her life is an infringement upon her Constitutional rights; so the court will determine what are the bounds of life, liberty, and security.

7. The Rodrigues case is of national importance, for it affects the issues of how terminally ill people can die in Canada.

8. She has difficulty swallowing food, and she needs help with many day-to-day activities.

9. Her speech and mobility have deteriorated; yet, her handicap and emotional depression will linger.

10. With science, and medicine there is hope; but the lawyers, and judges are deliberating cautiously.

The Careful Eye

Answers – Compound Sentences

All changes in punctuation, either additions or deletions, are underlined. Any words that have been added appear in bold.

1. Sue Rodrigues wants to die with dignity, and her case is before the Supreme Court of Canada.

2. Mrs. Rodrigues would control the dying process, and **she would** activate any device.

3. She is waiting for a judgement, and **she is hoping for** an approval.

4. Suicide is not illegal in Canada, but helping someone to end her life is.

5. The moral and social issues make sense, **yet** the legalities do puzzle me.

6. Denying Mrs. Rodrigues control over her life is an infringement upon her Constitutional rights, so the court will determine what are the bounds of life, liberty, and security.

7. Original sentence is correct.

8. Original sentence is correct.

9. Her speech and mobility have deteriorated, yet her handicap and emotional depression will linger.

10. With science and medicine there is hope, but the lawyers and judges are deliberating cautiously.

The Careful Eye

Commas, semicolons, colons

1. Exercise A:
Correct the following sentences exclusively by using punctuation.

2. Exercise B:
Correct these sentences by using punctuation and co-ordinating or subordinating conjunctions.

Sentence Patterns

1. Greenpeace saves wales however a green peach is bad for you.

2. Politicians unlike environmentalists must love acid rain since they don't want to get rid of it.

3. The Brazilians who have the biggest producer of oxygen think the rest of the world looks like the Amazon.

4. Tarzan lord of the jungle will no longer have trees from which to swing. Ah Jane.

5. The basis of forest life is being destroyed acid rain removes the nutrients from the top soil.

6. Frank Zappa's playing is not technically dazzling although many guitarists consider him the best.

7. Zappa enjoys Gail's muffins and St. Alphonzo's pancakes.

8. Zappa also enjoys blue hair cosmic debris Flo and Eddie and dumb social issues in the news.

9. Zappa chose Chad Wackerman out of hundreds of drummers agreeing with Ike Willis that Wackerman was the best reader.

10. Zappa is an innovative composer some of his songs are two albums long.

11. There is only one thing Zappa really hates evangelists.

12. Zappa is interested in only two things Stravinsky and people who don't register to vote.

13. Cliff Brown was technically a superb musician however he was a lousy driver.

The Careful Eye

14. Mozart was a musical genius no one appreciated his music until he was dead.

15. Musicians who admire themselves vanish from the scene.

16. Johnny Coltrane was a great sax man but he couldn't crotchet as well as his grandmother.

17. Jaco Pastorius a virtuoso guitarist had three interests jazz late night talk shows and very dry martinis

18. There is one thing Jaco would not tolerate bad engineers.

19. Jaco is the complete professional he takes extra strength Tylenol for hangovers.

20. Jaco was an exceedingly fast bass player who could also read speedily.

21. Charlie Parker founding father of bebop played the alto sax because he abused drugs he died at an early age.

22. Because Leona Boyd is a virtuoso guartist she is in high demand on the concert stage.

23. The structure and harmonic scheme remain as fixed elements and the influence of the melody is often sensed even when it cannot be heard and isolated.

24. Well defined cadences separate some variations some are fused together while others are linked by cadenza like passages.

25. A partita originally was a set of variations but in the seventeenth and eighteenth centuries the term came to be used interchangeably with suite serenade and cassation are names which suggest performance out of doors.

The Careful Eye

Answers Exercise A:

1. Greenpeace saves whales; however, a green peach is bad for you.

2. Politicians, unlike environmentalists, must love acid rain since they don't want to get rid of it.

3. The Brazilians, who have the biggest producer of oxygen, think the rest of the world looks like the Amazon.

4. Tarzan, lord of the jungle, will no longer have trees from which to swing. Ah Jane!

5. The basis of forest life is being destroyed; acid rain removes the nutrients from the top soil.

6. Frank Zappa's playing is not technically dazzling, although many guitarists consider him the best.

7. Zappa enjoys Gail's muffins and St. Alphonzo's pancakes.

8. Zappa also enjoys blue hair, cosmic debris, Flo and Eddie, and dumb social issues in the news.

9. Zappa chose Chad Wackerman out of hundreds of drummers, agreeing with Ike Willis that Wackerman was the best reader.

10. Zappa is an innovative composer; some of his songs are two albums long.

11. There is only one thing Zappa really hates: evangelists.

12. Zappa is interested in only two things: Stravinsky and people who don't register to vote.

13. Cliff Brown was technically a superb musician; however, he was a lousy driver.

14. Mozart was a musical genius; no one appreciated his music until he was dead.

15. Musicians who admire themselves vanish from the scene.

16. Johnny Coltrane was a great sax man, but he couldn't crotchet as well as his grandmother.

17. Jaco Pastorius, a virtuoso guitarist, had three interests: jazz, late

The Careful Eye

night talk shows, and very dry martinis.

18. There is one thing Jaco would not tolerate — bad engineers.

19. Jaco is the complete professional: he takes extra-strength Tylenol for hangovers.

20. Jaco was an exceedingly fast bass player who could also read speedily.

21. Charlie Parker, founding father of bebop, played the alto sax; because he abused drugs, he died an early death.

22. Because Leona Boyd is a virtuoso guartist, she is in high demand on the concert stage.

23. The structure and harmonic scheme remain as fixed elements, and the influence of the melody is often sensed, even when it cannot be heard and isolated.

24. Well defined cadences separate some variations; some are fused together, while others are linked by cadenza-like passages.

25. A partita originally was a set of variations; but, in the seventeenth and eighteenth centuries, the term came to be used interchangeably with suite. Serenade and cassation are names which suggest performance out of doors.

Answers Exercise B:

1. Greenpeace saves whales, <u>yet</u> a green peach is bad for you.

2. Politicians, <u>not</u> environmentalists, must love acid rain since they don't want to get rid of it.

3. **While** the Brazilians have the biggest producer of oxygen, they think the rest of the world looks like the Amazon.

4. Tarzan, <u>although he is</u> lord of the jungle, will no longer have trees from which to swing. Ah Jane!

5. The basis of forest life is being destroyed, <u>for</u> acid rain removes the nutrients from the top soil.

6. Frank Zappa's playing is not technically dazzling, although many guitarists consider him the best.   **Correct**

The Careful Eye

7. Zappa enjoys Gail's muffins and St. Alphonzo's pancakes. **Correct**

8. Zappa also enjoys blue hair, cosmic debris, Flo and Eddie, and dumb social issues in the news. **Correct**

9. Zappa chose Chad Wackerman out of hundreds of drummers, <u>agreed</u> with Ike Willis that Wackerman was the best reader.

10. Because Zappa is an innovative composer, some of his songs are two albums long.

11. There is only one thing Zappa really hates,<u> and it is</u> evangelists.

12. Zappa is interested in only two things,<u> and they are</u> Stravinsky and people who don't register to vote.

13. Cliff Brown was technically a superb musician,<u> yet</u> he was a lousy driver.

14. Mozart was a musical genius,<u> but</u> no one appreciated his music until he was dead.

15. Musicians who admire themselves vanish from the scene. **Correct**

16. Johnny Coltrane was a great sax man, but he couldn't crotchet as well as his grandmother. **Correct**

17. <u>Although</u> Jaco Pastorius was a virtuoso guitarist,<u> he</u> had three interests: jazz, late night talk shows, and very dry martinis.

18. There is one thing Jaco would not tolerate,<u> and that was</u> bad engineers.

19. Jaco is the complete professional, but he takes extra-strength Tylenol for hangovers.

20. Jaco was an exceedingly fast bass player,<u> and he</u> could also read speedily.

21. Charlie Parker played the alto sax <u>and became the founding father of bebop.</u>

22. Because Leona Boyd is a virtuoso guitarist,<u> she</u> is in high demand on the concert stage.

23. <u>Because</u> the structure and harmonic scheme remain as fixed elements, and the influence of the melody is often sensed, even

The Careful Eye

when it cannot be heard and isolated.

24. Well defined cadences separate some variations,_ and_ some are fused together, while others are linked by cadenza-like passages.

25. A partita originally was a set of variations; but, in the seventeenth and eighteenth centuries, the term came to be used interchangeably with "_suite_". Serenade and cassation are names which suggest performance out of doors.

The Careful Eye

Run-ons, comma splices, commas

Correct the misuse of run-ons, comma splices, and commas within the following article.

Jean's Lessons in Learning

There were, indeed, some surprises in store for me at college attendance at a post-secondary institution was not approached lightly; quite frankly, I was in awe of academia in spite of that, I recognized that the studies would require diligence and hard work; I was fully prepared to exert at least twice the effort that I perceived the "normal" student required in return I expected to be excited enthralled and even mesmerized by the new world of ideas that would open up to me my motivation you see was not external, in terms of grades, or job training. I was captivated by the mystique of acquiring knowledge; I longed to taste the forbidden fruit of different belief systems, philosophies, and alternative lifestyles. It, was therefore with anticipation, that I approached the beginning of the course of my choice, Comparative Religions 146.

What caught me off guard was the panic that gripped me at my first class! Many of the words uttered by the professor were foreign to me I asked for the spelling of one of those words — dichotomy — and then headed for a session with the dictionary. The entire course followed that pattern yes my expectations were fulfilled. The professor brought to life other belief systems, and engendered in me a craving for an even deeper understanding. However my lack of vocabulary sophistication was all too evident I

The Careful Eye

accepted this deficiency, somewhat shakily, as a lesson in itself and the desire to overcome it spurred me on to even more adventures in learning.

Quite apart from the struggle to acquire a new vocabulary there was another somewhat hidden lesson — learning to learn I came to view this process as continuous one that now colours my whole attitude to life and learning long after the excitement and wonder of Comparative Religions 146 have faded.

Answers – Run-ons, comma splices, commas

Underlining has been used to indicate a change, either addition or deletion of one or more marks of punctuation.

There were, indeed, some surprises in store for me at college. Attendance at a post-secondary institution was not approached lightly; quite frankly, I was in awe of academia. In spite of that, I recognized that the studies would require diligence and hard work; I was fully prepared to exert at least twice the effort that I perceived the "normal" student required. In return, I expected to be excited, enthralled, and even mesmerized by the new world of ideas that would open up to me. My motivation, you see, was not external, in terms of grades or job training. I was captivated by the mystique of acquiring knowledge; I longed to taste the forbidden fruit of different belief systems, philosophies, and alternative lifestyles. It was, therefore, with anticipation that I approached the beginning of the course of my choice — Comparative Religions 146.

What caught me off guard was the panic that gripped me at my first class! Many of the words uttered by the professor were foreign to me. I asked for the spelling of one of those words — dichotomy — and then headed for a session with the dictionary. The entire course followed that pattern. Yes, my expectations were fulfilled. The professor brought to life other belief systems and engendered in me a craving for an even deeper understanding. However, my lack of vocabulary sophistication was all too evident. I accepted this deficiency, somewhat shakily, as a lesson in itself, and the desire to overcome it spurred me on to even more adventures in learning.

Quite apart from the struggle to acquire a new vocabulary, there was another, somewhat hidden lesson — learning to learn. I came to view this process as continuous, one that now colours my whole attitude to life and learning, long after the excitement and wonder of Comparative Religions 146 have faded.

The Careful Eye

Phrases, Clauses

Identify the fifteen underlined words, phrases, or clauses as adjectives, adverbs, infinitives, nouns, prepositions, or verbs.

English: The Key to Jobs for Immigrants

Over the past few years, there has been a considerable shift in the make-up of our society. A greater percentage <u>of the population</u>[1] consists of immigrants from countries where the primary language of communication is not English. Previously, many of these immigrants were content to work at jobs <u>where English-speaking skills were not required.</u>[2] However, this situation <u>has changed drastically</u>[3] in recent years.

The economy is now in recession. The key to employment and economic survival is the <u>ability to communicate effectively in English.</u>[4] The present state of the economy, <u>having resulted in fewer factory jobs</u>[5], has closed retail stores and filled classrooms. Especially <u>strained</u>[6] are the English-language classes where students hope <u>to gain the needed skills</u>[7] to help them acquire employment. English as a second language is a program designed to help immigrants who have <u>a language other than English as their mother tongue.</u>[8] Most of these immigrants depended previously on factory jobs where proficiency is English communication was not required. With the loss of many of these factory jobs, the unemployed immigrants are finding it increasingly difficult to obtain alternative employment without English proficiency. Many of these immigrants are returning to school to improve their English language skills. Many others are unable to obtain admission to classes because of a lack of government funding for the classes.[9] The requirement for English language instruction has grown in reverse to the government's ability to provide it. Government has lost tax revenues from businesses that have failed[10] and from employees who are no longer working.[11] More immigrants are going to school, requiring English-language courses[12], and preparing for employment.[13]

With the advancements in technology, employees need to be proficient in the English language[14]; unfortunately, most immigrants whose mother tongue is not English are not. Government needs to provide the facilities and programs[15] to enable these immigrants to be active in the labour force.

Answers – Phrases, Clauses:

1. prepositional phrase
2. noun clause
3. verb phrase
4. noun clause
5. verbal (adjective)
6. adjective complement
7. infinitive clause
8. adjective clause
9. adverb clause
10. adjective clause
11. adjective clause
12. adjective complement
13. adjective complement
14. infinitive phrase
15. infinitive phrase

The Careful Eye

Apostrophes

> Apostrophes have been used incorrectly in the following article. Eliminate the incorrectly used ones, and add apostrophes to words that require them.

Without Advertising

Can you imagine a world without advertising? Its pretty difficult, isn't it? Advertising is ubiquitous. Its obvious and its subliminal. So are its effects. It can be informative and entertaining; it can be misleading and insulting.

The type of advertising to be most wary of is the "lifestyle" ad. Usually shown are young, sexy men and women having immense fun and pleasure, the direct result of using the advertisers product. One can be simultaneously amused and concerned about the woman in the shower rubbing her body with Dial soap; she's obviously in a state of intense pleasure and excitement. It appears that shes rubbing her body with some powerful feel-good drug as well as washing her armpits. Whats in that soap?

Advertising has moved to the point where I have enormous trouble distinguishing products: Swatch (watch), Jaguar (automobile), Sensodyne (toothpaste), Beechnut (gum), Levis (jeans), Seager Method (hair transplant), and a rub on your furry little tummy (Bell Telephone). Ads, ads, ads --- they're all the same to look at, and their message is the same: buy these products and you'll be young, sexy, and vibrant. Buy the products and you'll be exactly like those who model them.

The Careful Eye

Sexual stereotyping and innuendo are used to sell almost anything. If you buy a new car, sultry women in diaphanous evening gowns leading panthers on diamond leashes will be yours'. Merely by buying this product, you can change the type of person you are. Whether or not we approve, this type of message influence's us and our children. We are told to measure self-worth by the brand of product's that we purchase. Is one less worthy as a man if he drink's Labatt's Blue rather than Budweiser or drives a Cherokee van rather than a Sovereign? Are you worthless as a stereotyped "wife" because your washing isn't "whiter than white," because your dishes aren't "squeaky clean," because your lipstick and nail polish aren't the colour of moondrops'?

Advertisings silly messages' are pushed at us relentlessly on television and billboard's, in magazines and newspapers, on the side's of buses, in the subways, on the radio, in elevators, everywhere! It's doing more than informing us about the value and desirability of "irresistible" products. Advertisers' woo our dollars by influencing our perception of the value and desirability of ourselves. Therein lies the danger. Advertising's appeal is powerful, glamorous, seductive. Billions of dollars are spent promoting products, most of which didn't exist one hundred years ago and most of which we don't need now. We've contributed to our environments fragility and our ozone layers depletion. Why do we let advertising's effect determine our self-worth?

Answers – Apostrophes
NOTE: All additions or deletions of apostrophes are in bold type.

Can you imagine a world without advertising? **It's** pretty difficult, isn't it? Advertising is ubiquitous. **It's** obvious and **it's** subliminal. So are its effects. It can be informative and entertaining; it can be misleading and insulting.

The type of advertising to be most wary of is the "lifestyle" ad. Usually shown are young, sexy men and women having immense fun and pleasure, the direct result of using the advertise**r's** product. One can be simultaneously amused and concerned about the woman in the shower rubbing her body with Dial soap; sh**e's** obviously in a state of intense pleasure and excitement. It appears that she's rubbing her body with some powerful feel-good drug as well as washing her armpits. Wha**t's** in that soap?

Advertising has moved to the point where I have enormous trouble distinguishing products: Swatch (watch), Jaguar (automobile), Sensodyne (toothpaste), Beechnut (gum), Levis (jeans), Seager Method (hair transplant), and a rub on your furry little tummy (Bell Telephone). Ads, ads, ads — they're all the same to look at, and their message is the same: buy these products and you'll be young, sexy, and vibrant. Buy the products and you'll be exactly like those who model them.

Sexual stereotyping and innuendo are used to sell almost anything. If you buy a new car, sultry women in diaphanous evening gowns leading panthers on diamond leashes will be y**ours**. Merely by buying this product, you can change the type of person you are. Whether or not we approve, this type of message influ**ences** us and our children. We are told to measure self-worth by the brand of produ**cts** that we purchase. Is one less worthy as a man if he drinks Labatt's Blue rather than Budweiser or drives a Cherokee van rather than a Sovereign? Are you worthless as a stereotyped "wife" because your washing isn't "whiter than white," because your dishes aren't "squeaky clean," because your lipstick and nail polish aren't the colour of moondrops?

Advertisin**g's** silly messa**ges** are pushed at us relentlessly on television and billbo**ards**, in magazines and newspapers, on the **sides** of buses, in the subways, on the radio, in elevators, everywhere! It's doing more than informing us about the value and desirability of "irresistible" products. Advertise**rs** woo our dollars by influencing our perception of the value and desirability of ourselves. Therein lies the danger. Advertising's appeal is powerful, glamorous, seductive. Billions of dollars are spent promoting products, most of which didn't exist one hundred years ago and most of which we don't need now. We've contributed to our environm**ent's** fragility and our ozone lay**er's** depletion. Why do we let advertising's effect determine our self-worth?

The Careful Eye

Commas

> Without deleting or adding any words or phrases, insert 15 commas to punctuate the following paragraphs correctly.

Mumbo-jumbo on Curriculum

An article in The Toronto Star October 24 1992 says that education critics are opposed to a new curriculum policy for Ontario schools. Critics call the document "vague and rhetorical" but perhaps they are not giving the proposal a chance.

This document which is presently confidential is still being drafted. Opponents to the proposal should consider this fact before they begin tearing apart ideas that have not yet had a chance for revision. To unleash a scathing attack on this draft without allowing its creators an opportunity to defend themselves a typical over-reactive response is the epitome of prejudice and of logical fallacy.

The critics have taken this opportunity to expound upon what they feel are the negative aspects of the policy and they ignore the greater goals. The four principles are excellence equity accountability and partnership in education. These a person would think are quite admirable ideals in education. This is a wide range for curriculum.

To reject this proposal without having it presented in its completed form is questionable. If any opposition to this policy is warranted then all parties who have had an opportunity to examine and review the perspective outline should be involved in its ratification. The rejection of the new curriculum policy by a handful of dissenters who do not necessarily have all the facts should not be taken too seriously.

Answers – Commas:
Underlining indicates where changes have been made.

An article in *The Toronto Star*, October 24, 1992, says that education critics are opposed to a new curriculum policy for Ontario schools. Critics call the document "vague and rhetorical" but perhaps they are not giving the proposal a chance.

This document, which is presently confidential, is still being drafted. Opponents to the proposal should consider this fact before they begin tearing apart ideas that have not yet had a chance for revision. To unleash a scathing attack on this draft without allowing its creators an opportunity to defend themselves, a typical over-reactive response, is the epitome of prejudice and of logical fallacy.

The critics have taken this opportunity to expound upon what they feel are the negative aspects of the policy, and they ignore the greater goals. The four principles are excellence, equity, accountability, and partnership in education. These, a person would think, are quite admirable ideals in education. This is a wide range for curriculum.

To reject this proposal without having it presented in its completed form is questionable. If any opposition to this policy is warranted, then all parties who have had an opportunity to examine and review the perspective outline should be involved in its ratification. The rejection of the new curriculum policy by a handful of dissenters who do not necessarily have all the facts should not be taken too seriously.

The Careful Eye

Pronoun Antecedents

Underline the correct pronoun from the choices given and circle its antecedent.

Save the Roaches

John and Janet were getting disgusted with *(his or her, their)* apartment. Neither Mr. Hand, the superintendent, nor *(his, their)* helpers were doing *(his, their)* jobs properly. As a result, everyone in the building was complaining because *(he or she, they)* did not have enough heat in *(his or her, their)* apartment. Since many of the burned-out lights had not be replaced in the lobby, one of the tenants, Ms. Foot, tripped in the dark and hurt *(she, her, their)* back. The filthy hallways were enough to make every person in the building sick to *(his or her, their)* stomach. To make matters worse, people could not get anything repaired in *(his or her, their)* apartments. Each of the tenants complained, but the landlord, Mr. Head, paid no attention to *(him or her, them)*. Therefore, the unhappy residents of the building formed *(his or her, their)* own tenants' association to pressure the landlord. It was clear that either the tenants or the landlord would have *(his or her, his, her, their)* way. On several occasions, the association presented *(its, it's, their)* demands, but the landlord ignored *(it, them)*. At this point, John and Janet decided to move, but first *(he or she, they)* had one small matter to take care of. To get even with *(his or her, their)* landlord, *(he or she, they)* placed a newspaper advertisement that read: "Wanted—2000 live cockroaches. We are willing to pay top dollar for *(it, them)*. Call 675-6622." The first person to call was a Ms. Finger, who said that *(he or she, he, she, them)* wanted to know why John and Janet needed 2000 live cockroaches. John happily explained, "Our lease requires us to leave the apartment exactly as we found *(it, them)*, and that's just what we intend to do!"

Answers – Pronoun Antecedents
The correct pronoun from the choices given is underlined, and its antecedent has been bolded.

John and Janet were getting disgusted with *(his or her, their)* apartment. Neither **Mr. Hand**, the superintendent, nor *(his, their)* **helpers** were doing *(his, their)* jobs properly. As a result, **everyone** in the building was complaining because *(he or she, they)* did not have enough heat in *(his or her, their)* apartment. Since many of the burned-out lights had not be replaced in the lobby, one of the tenants, **Ms. Foot**, tripped in the dark and hurt *(she, her, their)* back. The filthy hallways were enough to make every **person** in the building sick to *(his or her, their)* stomach. To make matters worse, **people** could not get anything repaired in *(his or her, their)* apartments. **Each** of the tenants complained, but the landlord, Mr. Head, paid no attention to *(him or her, them)*. Therefore, the unhappy **residents** of the building formed *(his or her, their)* own tenants' association to pressure the landlord. It was clear that either the tenants or the **landlord** would have *(his or her, his, her, their)* way. On several occasions, the **association** presented *(its, it's, their)* **demands**, but the landlord ignored *(it, them)*. At this point, **John and Janet** decided to move, but first *(he or she, they)* had one small matter to take care of. To get even with *(his or her, their)* landlord, *(he or she, they)* placed a newspaper advertisement that read: "Wanted—2000 live cockroaches. We are willing to pay top dollar for *(it, them)*. Call 675-6622." The first person to call was a **Ms. Finger**, who said that *(he or she, he, she, them)* wanted to know why John and Janet needed 2000 live cockroaches. John happily explained, "Our lease requires us to leave the **apartment** exactly as we found *(it, them)*, and that's just what we intend to do!"

The Careful Eye

Person Shifts

This article contains shifts in person. Remove the faulty, unnecessary shifts, correct the verbs, and then make the article consistent from the following points of view. Note that **he/she** becomes unnecessarily repetitive; **they** is the most readable; and, **one** creates great distance between the reader and the speaker. Either **he** or **she** exclusively is currently considered sexist.
a. Third person singular masculine (he)
b. Third person singular feminine (she)
c. Third person singular, common gender (he/she)
d. Third person plural (they)
e. Third person singular formal (one)

Retirement

People who plan their retirement do not experience the same hardships as those who do not. It seems that some form of preparation should be undertaken before retirement to relieve financial and social preparation.

When a person retires, the monthly or weekly cheque no longer enters the home. If you have not planned for retirement, you may have to exist on old age pensions which in many cases are just barely sufficient for survival. Those who have planned for retirement will have a nest egg stashed away in the form of an R.R.S.P or a large bank account to withdraw from.

Our social life is also affected by retirement. After retirement we find ourselves losing contact with our former associates from work. Those who have revolved their social life around work will find themselves without friends as interests will change. Friends outside the workplace should therefore have been established.

Our identity can be affected. By losing our job, losing our friends, and feeling we don't belong, a person's self-worth can be affected. Upon retiring, if your leisure and work times are planned, you can overcome this. Those who have continued their outside interests will find their day most satisfying.

Planning for retirement can help overcome some of the hardships that retired people must face.

Answers – Person Shifts
*This answer is provided from the **third person singular feminine** point of view. The verbs have been changed accordingly.*

She who plans her retirement does not experience the same hardships as women who do not. It seems that some form of preparation should be undertaken before retirement to relieve financial and social preparation.

When a woman retires, the monthly or weekly cheque no longer enters the home. If she has not planned for retirement, she may have to exist on old age pensions which in many cases are just barely sufficient for survival. She who has planned for retirement will have a nest egg stashed away in the form of an R.R.S.P or a large bank account to withdraw from.

Her social life is also affected by retirement. After retirement she finds herself losing contact with her former associates from work. She who has revolved her social life around work will find herself without friends as interests will change. Friends outside the workplace should therefore have been established.

Her identity can be affected. By losing her job, losing her friends, and feeling she doesn't belong, her self-worth can be affected. Upon retiring, if her leisure and work times are planned, she can overcome this dilemma. She who has continued her outside interests will find her day most satisfying.

Planning for retirement can help overcome some of the hardships that a retired woman must face.

The Careful Eye

Verbals

1. Identify the eighteen underlined verbals in the following article as present participles, past participles, gerunds, or infinitives.
2. State whether each verbal is used as an adjective, adverb, or noun.
   NOTE: Participles are adjectives; gerunds are nouns; infinitives are adjectives, adverbs, or nouns. **Verbals are never verbs in sentences.**

Bohdan's Munch

Edvard Munch's The Scream (1893) presents an intensely emotional work, filled with pathos and despair[1], and, most of all, realism. The character in the foreground — possibly a woman — appears distraught, with her hands folded[2] in an "oh-my-God" desperate position. The eyes, mouth, in fact the entire face and posture, suggest a woman having trouble[3] coping with her situation.[4] Several themes are clear in this painting. The couple in the background, unaffected by the plight of the woman in the foreground[5], appear to be casually walking away[6], overlooking the port.[7] This situation displays their indifference to the woman's cry, perhaps symbolizing a desensitized, inhumane attitude toward the problems of one less fortunate than they. Against this background of darkness and gloom, despair and morbidity, the expression on the woman's face is unsettling.[8] Although she is not directly looking at the viewers, she appears to be crying out to us obliquely[9], to take pity upon her.[10] People usually cry out for help. The Scream is a work of art that seems to appeal to our emotions[11], touching on the darkness and despair[12] that we all feel at times. This woman is alone with her problems, as we too can feel alone in an uncaring, indifferent world. Madness, like death, must ultimately be faced alone.

This painting stands as a juxtaposition of the problems of the individual, <u>layered upon the background of an oblivious world</u>[13]; it is realism accompanied by an artistic touch of timid Impressionism. Munch's <u>pending</u>[14] nervous breakdown seems already forecast in this scene; even the landscape's highly expressive form is saturated with dull colours. <u>Spoken</u>[15] words are naturally retained with much more difficulty than those we read; but, while well-trained listeners can reproduce amazing amounts of conversation, those who read faces accurately are the most astute of all, <u>having understood the emotion</u>[16], and <u>giving concrete form to it</u>.[17] <u>Being profoundly affected by the death of his mother and of two of his sisters</u>[18], this Norwegian painter succeeds in presenting "the solitary crowd" where death, pain, and sickness are ever-present, even to people in love.

Answers – Verbals

1. filled with pathos and despair (past part, adj.)
2. folded (past part, adj.)
3. having trouble (pres part, adj.)
4. coping with her situation (pres part, adj.)
5. unaffected by the plight of the woman in the foreground (pres part, adj.)
6. to be casually walking away (infinitive, adv.)
7. overlooking the port (pres part, adj.)
8. unsettling (gerund, noun)
9. to be crying out to us obliquely (infinitive, adv.)
10. to take pity upon her (infinitive, adv.)
11. to appeal to our emotions (infinitive, noun)
12. touching on the darkness and despair (pres part, adj.)
13. layered upon the background of an oblivious world (past part, adj.)
14. pending (gerund, adj.)
15. Spoken (past part, adj.)
16. having understood the emotion (pres part, adj.)
17. giving concrete form to it (pres part, adj.)
18. Being profoundly affected by the death of his mother and of two of his sisters (pres part, adj.)

The Careful Eye

Verbals

> 1. Identify at least eighteen verbals — gerunds, infinitives, participles — in the following article.
> 2. State the kind of verbal used.
> 3. Name the part of speech to indicate how the verbal is used.

Speyside Fred

Having grown up in a small town outside Toronto, I have always enjoyed the city. My home town, Speyside, was a dot on a map that offered little to an adolescent who craved excitement. Although now that I look back, I admit that I miss the community, and I long to return some day.

Toronto and Speyside have similarities that will never escape me. No matter where I live in Canada, the cost of living is high as it is in both of these places. A person might believe that living in the country would mean lower living costs; but, on the whole, whether buying produce from a store or buying feed for livestock, the costs are about the same.

Fortunately, no matter where I live, making friends seems easy. Friends I have made in Toronto do not differ much from those whom I had in Speyside. Each weekend now my Torontonian friends and I redefine the word "boring" and wonder why we thought life in the city used to be so exciting. I guess that people raised in either Toronto or Speyside carry this genetic dysfunction.

Furthermore, I have found, to my surprise, many wildlife. There is not the abundance in the big city that there is in Speyside, but they do exist if you look for them. Just walk out any night before garbage day and you're bound to find a rummaging raccoon or a slinking skunk, both bigger and bolder than any rural co-species.

Many things displease me or distress me in Toronto — the crime rate for one, which is mostly caused by overpopulation — is out of control. I would never lock my car or house in Speyside, but in overcrowded, civilized Toronto I am forced to practise this ritual of paranoia.

In sleeping Speyside, there is always a feeling of town unity. If my neighbour needs to bring in his hay, I am willing to help, and I offer to do so, knowing he would gladly return the favour for any neighbour or for me. In Toronto, if I even say hello to my neighbour (what's his name?), I am bound to get a cold stare; while in Speyside, a "countrified" neighbour would drive or even walk two miles to say "Hi".

I am quite happy living in Toronto where I'm close to everything and where housing is affordable. Some day if I need to reshape my life I will endeavour to persuade myself again to live in the country where the air is moderately clean, the crime rate is low, and the people are friendly.

The Careful Eye

Answers – Verbals

1. Having grown up in a small town outside Toronto (pres. part adj.)
2. living in the country (gerund, noun)
3. buying produce from a store (gerund, noun)
4. buying feed for livestock (gerund, noun)
5. making friends (gerund, noun)
6. exciting (gerund, noun)
7. to find a rummaging raccoon (infinitive noun)
8. rummaging raccoon (pres. part, adj.)
9. slinking skunk (pres. part, adj.)
10. overcrowded (past part, adj.)
11. civilized (past part, adj.)
12. to practise this ritual (infinitive, noun)
13. sleeping (pres. part, adj.)
14. to do so (infinitive, noun)
15. knowing he would return the favour (pres. part, adj.)
16. to get a cold stare (infinitive, noun)
17. countrified (past part, adj.)
18. living in Toronto (pres. part, adj.)
19. to reshape my life (infinitive, noun)
20. to persuade myself (infinitive, noun)
21. to live in the country (infinitive, noun)

Sentence Construction

Compose the sentences according to the required grammatical construction.

Application

1. A simple sentence with one co-ordinating conjunction joining three gerunds.
2. A simple sentence joining three prepositional phrases.
3. A compound sentence using two prepositional phrases in each independent clause.
4. A compound sentence using a co-ordinating conjunction showing contrast.
5. A compound sentence using a conjunctive adverb showing contrast.
6. A compound sentence using a conjunctive adverb showing result.
7. A compound sentence using a conjunctive adverb showing restatement or clarification.
8. A simple sentence using a correlative conjunction showing addition.
9. A simple sentence using a correlative conjunction showing separation.
10. A simple sentence using a correlative conjunction showing negative separation.
11. A simple sentence using "not only".
12. A complex sentence using any subordinating conjunction introducing a terminal dependent clause.
13. A complex sentence using the subordinating conjunction "in order that".
14. A complex sentence using the subordinating conjunction "provided".
15. A compound-complex sentence using three introductory clauses beginning with "unless".
16. A simple sentence using three gerund phrases.
17. A compound-complex sentence using two dependent clauses interrupting one of the independent clauses.
18. A compound sentence using a conjunctive adverb showing result.
19. A complex sentence using both an introductory dependent and terminal dependent clause.
20. A simple sentence using only one word.

The Careful Eye

Answers – Sentence Construction

1
2
3
4
5
6
7
8
9
10
11
12
13
14
15
16

The Careful Eye

17 _____

18 _____

19 _____

20 _____

The Careful Eye

Sentences: Codes Applied

> Compose the following sentences according to the requirements using the subjects indicated in brackets.
> *NOTE: This exercise reinforces your understanding of sentence patterns and components.*

1. A complex sentence with one adverb clause answering "why". (studying for exams)
2. A complex sentence with one adjective clause modifying the subject and one adverb clause modifying the verb. (men with 'beer' bellies)
3. A sentence with one noun clause as noun complement. (minority rights)
4. A sentence with one noun clause as subject. (the ozone problem)
5. A compound-complex sentence with one adjective clause and one adverb clause. (rain forest)
6. A compound-complex sentence with two adverb clauses. (NAFTA)
7. A complex sentence with one adjective clause and one adverb clause. (environment)
8. A complex sentence with two adjective clauses. (higher education)
9. A compound sentence with three independent clauses. (standardized testing in schools)
10. A sentence with one noun clause as subject. (academic expectations)
11. A complex sentence with three introductory noun clauses. (Brent Carver and The Kiss of the Spider Woman)
12. A simple sentence with three prepositional phrases. (unemployment rates)
13. A simple sentence with three prepositional phrases and the subject implied. (food banks)
14. A complex sentence using whoever. (smoking law reform)
15. A compound sentence with two implied subjects. (sexual harassment)
16. A compound complex sentence using whomever. (Young Offenders Act)
17. A simple sentence with a gerund phrase as subject. (horoscopes)
18. A simple sentence with an infinitive phrase. (Toronto Blue Jays)
19. A simple sentence with absolute phrase. (Montreal Canadiens)
20. A compound sentence with two infinitive phrases. (single parents)
21. A compound sentence with gerund phrases as both subjects. (SkyDome)
22. A compound-complex sentence using a conjunction of exception. (Edmonton Oilers)
23. A complex sentence with an essential noun clause separating subject and verb. (refugees)
24. A complex sentence with an adverb clause at the end. (computers in business)
25. A simple sentence using only one word. (optional subject choice)

The Careful Eye

1. Because I had a lot of studing, I studied all weekend.
2. Men, who have beer bellies,
3. This is what she said.
4. What is happening to the ozone is a big problem.
5. When people do not destroy it, the rainforest, which is beautiful, can benefit us.
6.
7.
8.
9.
10.
11.
12.
13.
14.

The Careful Eye

15.

16.

17.

18.

19.

20.

21.

22.

23.

24.

25.

Section III
Editing and Proofreading
Level I

The Careful Eye

Answers are not provided for the excercises in this section. They are intended to be marked by the instructor, or taken up for correction by the entire class.

Fragments

Proofread the following letter by eliminating all sentence fragments.

Hammacher

Welcome to Hammacher. For 142 years, Hammacher has been a seemingly contradictory combination of innovation and tradition. Our products represent the best of the past and the inventiveness of the future.

We have always stood for quality. In the products we sell and in the attention we give our customers. We are sending you our new catalogue. With the hope that once you've browsed through it, you will become a Hammacher customer. A very special person, indeed.

Sincerely,

Jason X. Kennethauer
President

The Careful Eye

Fragments

1. On a separate sheet of paper, list the fragments in the following paragraph.
2. Correct all fragments by using punctuation to join them to complete, main ideas.

Telecommunicators

Someday soon you may not have to get up in the morning and go to work. You will work at home in front of your very own computer. Already several hundred thousand workers are telecommunicators. Doing at home what they used to do at the office. For instance one at-home secretary takes dictation from her boss over the telephone. Typing the letters directly on her computer terminal. Stockbrokers and salespersonnel can place orders and keep records right in their living rooms. All they need is a computer hook-up. A few banks and consulting firms give their employees a choice of working in the office or working at home. Many other businesses are considering trying this idea. Some women with small children are attracted to the idea of telecommuting. Although others prefer a job that gets them out of the house. To provide some time away from the children, at least for a few hours a day. Telecommuting does have many advantages though. Including no commuting time, no expensive lunch hours, and an extra income tax deduction for a home office. It is also nice to work without direct supervision. Knowing that the boss is not looking over your shoulder. Perhaps that is the greatest advantage of all.

The Careful Eye

Run-ons

1. Read the following unpunctuated paragraph.
2. Determine which ideas belong together.
3. Determine which ideas could be subordinated by adding co-ordinating or subordinating conjunctions; note which ones are best left as principal ideas.
4. Make all necessary corrections in punctuation.

Prince Edward Island Village

When I think of my happy years growing up on a mixed farm in rural Prince Edward Island I feel sentimental now for those times people cared for one another there they accepted the odd the old and the disabled women in the community baked pies cakes and bread at least twice a week and shared it with their relatives who would just drop in for supper they invited the minister either United Church or Baptist to Sunday supper people grew old they lived with one of their children on the homestead no one went to an old age home or a nursing home for there were none many people in my farming village had their grandparents or a spinster aunt living with them the lame the arthritic and the odd lived with their families too they were always part of the community I can never return to that farm to live but if I could I would like to replace the party telephone line with private lines that would alter their way of life.

Parallelism

PART A
Note the common denominators — repeated words, phrases or clauses in the following sentences.

1. He is the kind of employee who takes pride in his work, who intends to rise in the organization, and who allows nothing to stand in his way.

2. She wanted to protest strongly, to tell him what she thought, to transfer to another branch and never come back.

3. They went to Niagara Falls, to Fenlon Falls, to Quebec City.

4. He felt that Mary, since her promotion, had changed, that she had moved into another world, and that she had left him behind.

5. If we are to balance, if we are to have even the hope of balancing, we must "up" the computer.

6. To know you are honest is one thing; to prove it, quite another.

PART B
1. Whenever a sentence contains two or more similar items, these items must be kept grammatically parallel, regardless of how short they are or how long they are.

2. Change the following sentences so that all the elements are parallel.

1. She liked coffee breaks, telephone calls, subordinates, and going to workshops.

2. He was lazy, good-humoured, likeable, and sort of a crook.

3. She worked steadily but in a great big hurry.

4. She counted her cash, registered the total, and her nameplate was checked.

5. He was an expert accountant and could also write memos.

The Careful Eye

6. He was intelligent and a very dull employee.

7. Her ambition was to move to Kingston and transferring into Personnel work.

8. She wanted either money or to be promoted.

9. The transfer into Mortgages had been both difficult and a great trauma.

10. He wanted to pour all his efforts into the job, to do it well, but keeping the time down as much as possible.

11. Either I'm always in debt or in trouble.

12. She is the kind of woman who will neither change her mind nor her techniques.

13. Neither did the parents nor the students understand the education process.

14. Rumpole was boisterous, spoke too loudly, and demanded assistance from "she who must be obeyed".

15. To hear Eugen Gmeiner play organ is hearing the best of Bach interpreters.

PART C
Identify the correct sentence in the pairs provided.

1. a. I expected him to be angry and to reprimand her.

   b. I expected him to be angry and that he would scold her.

2. a. Which duty do you prefer—typing, filing, or to take dictation?

   b. Which duty do you prefer—typing, filing, or taking dictaion?

3. a. Be sure that all corrections appear not only on the originals, but also that all copies are correct too.

   b. Be sure that all corrections appear not only on the originals, but also on all copies.

4. a. A good personality is of value in business and in social situations.

   b. A good persoanlity is of value both in business and you need one too in social situations.

5. a. Good typing is one thing, but accurate wordprocessing is quite another.

   b. Good typing is one thing, but to operate a word processor is difficult.

6. a. Mr. Olsen either wants Agnes or me to take the message.

   b. Mr. Olsen wants either Agnes or me to take the message.

7. a. Not only had the office been cleaned but also freshly painted.

   b. The office had been not only cleaned but also freshly painted.

8. a. It is not possible to operate a switchboard if you are less than five feet tall or with a short reach.

   b. It is not possible to operate a switchboard if you are less than five feet tall or if you have a short reach.

9. a. In the fall, is your area well heated and with plenty of ventilation?

   b. In the fall, is your area well heated and well ventilated?

10. a. She said that Mr. Park had been preparing the payroll, and you should talk to him.

    b. She said that Mr. Park had been preparing the payroll and that you should talk with him.

The Careful Eye

> **PART D**
> 1. Each of the sentences below contains faulty parallelism. Make the appropriate grammatical corrections.
>
> 2. **NOTE:** In each sentence, one change will usually suffice, but occasionally you can make two changes in the sentence to keep the third element.

1. She planned a seminar at Waterloo, a six-week summer school at U. of T., and getting an M.B.A, at Western.

2. The manager was efficient, kind, and got along well with everyone.

3. He put away the cash neatly, accurately, and with a great deal of skill.

4. The boy wiped the telephones, cleaned off the counter tops, polished up the handle of the big front door, and even the skirtings were mopped.

5. Sam was a good typist and also kept house well.

6. The file clerk was efficient but an emotional person.

7. He hoped to be elected president of the C.A.A. or make the highest sales.

8. He was intelligent as well as having lots of friends.

9. He had to have the customer both contacted and to have her informed.

10. The things he looked forward to were lunchtime and leaving the office at five o'clock.

11. Either the women disliked or ignored her.

12. He enjoyed visiting the water cooler as well as trips to the washroom.

13. That man will neither take advice from his bosses nor his peers.

14. Their purpose was not only to take special courses in business but in art.

15. The committee is not only working hard to preserve efficient

routines but it is also working hard in adopting new systems.

16. They believe that the P.R. procedures will promote greater competition among branches, that they will enrich the lives of school children in the community, and will become major information dissemination centres.

17. Many employees believe that to be popular is happiness.

18. Study develops the mind; exercise develops the body; and understanding is developed by experience.

19. He made it clear, first, that he had no faith in the project; second, that he would not support it; and that, third, he would advise his colleagues against it.

20. They arrived for the opening of the SkyDome by bus, by train, by plane, and even walking.

PART E
Compose the following sentences as directed.

1. Complete the unfinished sentence below with three adjectival <u>who</u> clauses:

   He always made trouble; he was the kind of employee who...

2. Complete with a series of <u>infinitive phrases</u>, using a different verb for each phrase:

   To be promoted, she thought, she needed only to...

3. Using <u>to</u> as the preposition, complete this sentence with three prepositional phrases.

   In desperate search for a job, he went to...

The Careful Eye

4. Using <u>of</u> as the preposition, complete this sentence with three prepositional phrases:

   She was afraid of everything, of . . .

5. Complete this sentence with a series of <u>noun</u> clauses:

   He complained that the manager made too many demands, that. ..

6. Write a sentence beginning with three <u>adverbial</u> if clauses.

7. Write a different sentence ending with three <u>if</u> clauses.

8. Complete the sentence below by interrupting it with two parallel <u>if</u> clauses.

   The problem of staff relations, if. . ., and if. . ., must be solved.

9. Write a <u>balanced sentence</u>, such as the one below, but using different <u>infinitives</u>:

   If we are to remain united, if we are to have even the hope of remaining united, we must end political posturing and verbal diarrhea, and we must end them now.

The Careful Eye

General editing

> The following section contains numerous grammatical errors. Make corrections in the spaces <u>above</u> the errors. Insert punctuation where it should be.

The Great Mistake Hunt

Part I: The Beatles:

The Beatles are a group that influenced the history of popular music. From there early songs, like 'I Want to Hold your Hand', their brilliance was obvious; but there true genuis was revealed in the <u>Sergeant Pepper's Lonely Hearts Club Band</u> album.

Each one of the musicians had their own special appeal. Paul and John writes songs with alot of memorable lyrics. George: that later became involved with sitar music: also he wrote some important songs. Ringo; the drummer; didn't write two many songs; but he was an essential part of The Beatles sound.

It's to bad that you aren't old enough, to remember the excitement that The Beatles caused when it first became popular. When The Beatles appeared on "The Ed Sullivan Show": it launched their careers in North America. Everyone grew their hair long to copy The Beatles' style, boys were often thrown out of school for not getting hair cuts.

Although The Beatles became the idols of teenagers; the music was not popular with a large amount of adults. John Lennon said, 'We're more

123

The Careful Eye

popular than Jesus Christ'. This caused Beatles records to be banned in many places. Adults also worried that The Beatles hid secret messages in his songs; for example the short form LSD for the song <u>Lucy in the Sky with Diamonds</u>.

Irregardless of whether The Beatles were good role models, they will be remembered for along time. They're music is being performed by many other artists that recognize The Beatles' eternal appeal.

Part 2: Run-ons and Comma splices

Correct the run-on sentences and comma splices in the following article.

Tennis is a sport that has gained great popularity over the last ten years; both men and women enjoy it. Tennis courts are being built all over they can be found in cities, in the country, in the suburbs. People of all ages can play in fact some of the greatest players in the world are in their teens or early twenties. The most important and prestigious tournament is held every summer at Wimbledon, a suburb of London England however Canada's most important tournament is the Canadian Open it is, for now held at Glenn Abbey Oakville Ontario. One does not have to be a star athalete to enjoy tennis, it is great fun even for those who just want some fresh air and exercise.

The Careful Eye

Part 3: Misplaced Modifiers

Revise these three passages by correcting all sentences which contain misplaced modifiers.
> *NOTE: Move words or groups of words next to the noun they modify.*

A. I forgot to nearly send Christmas cards this year. All of my relatives would have been disappointed in other parts of the country. It really is not that much of a strain since I need to send about ten cards only. It is as easy as writing, "Hi, how are you?" and mailing it on a note in an envelope. I usually work from a list that I keep in my desk of friends' and relatives' names. I luckily remembered about the cards three days before the holiday; I just hope that too late I did not mail them.

B. Raising a family really is an easy task. Everyone thinks he knows the best way; anyone scarcely does it perfectly. Many people read Dr. Spock's book which presents clearly one accepted method. Everyone nearly has heard of that book at least. No matter what method they follow, parents are advised constantly to be kind and affectionate toward their children. Some parents say after the baby is born their lives are changed completely for the better. They don't mind if the baby cries even. They rock the baby pacing the floor back to sleep. They accept the trouble calmly, knowing the baby will outgrow soon that stage. If they have prepared themselves for the new arrival as they could early and completely, they are never really upset by the little problems that come up.

The Careful Eye

C. These days, many people are trying health foods in all parts of the country. The "Back to Nature" movement has nearly affected everyone in one way or another. Producers of health foods use no preservatives in their products which they claim are bad for the system. Cereals such as granola a totally natural food are especially popular. People are also eating unstarched rice which is supposed to be good for the digestive system particularly. Ice cream even comes in new natural flavours such as banana and coconut which is made with fresh bananas. Certainly health food companies are trying hard to attract customers interested in better nutrition.

Part 4: Dangling Modifiers

> Revise the following three passages by correcting all sentences which contain dangling modifiers.
> *NOTE: The subject and the modifier have to refer to the same person or thing.*

A. To throw a successful party, several factors must be taken into consideration. When making up a list of people to invite, they should be compatible. After deciding on the guests, the amount of food and drink must be decided. If preparing a fruit punch, a large bowl and ladle are necessary. To save money, fruit punch is often better than serving everyone cocktails. Preparing the food in advance is also a good idea. When planning the meal, the number of guests must, of course, be considered. By cooking ahead of time, a lot of bother may be avoided. To make a suggestion, lasagna is always a favourite. When a host serves punch and lasagna, you can be almost certain that the party will be successful.

B. As a way of fighting the high cost of travel and of conserving fuel, smaller automobiles are common. On the highway, mileage is improved in a small car. In the city, when driving in traffic, gasoline is saved. After an average of 10,000 kilometres of rollin' on the roads, the driver should bring his small car in for a tuneup. After receiving the proper care, any car owner will find that his vehicle is ready for continued, efficient use. When you think about it, the day of the big car, like the ozone layer, is gone.

C. On arriving at Pearson International Airport, the sights and sounds amazed Pierre. Having travelled alone, so many people hurrying around and shouting came as a jolt to him. Coming from a small village in the south of France, so much commotion had never before been witnessed by the young traveller. And being only eight years old and a bit nervous, his luggage seemed to be his only companion. On this trip, his cousins in Brampton would be his hosts. After looking for them at the gate, and not being able to find them, an attendant took him to the information booth. Over the loudspeaker, Pierre's cousins were paged. To locate them, an announcement had to be made twice by the attendant. Then, running through the terminal, from the other end of the building, Pierre recognized his relatives. Feeling relieved, Pierre ran to them and excaped the crazy crowds of Pearson International.

The Careful Eye

Part 5: Faulty pronoun references

Revise this passage by eliminating faulty pronoun references.

<u>A</u>. When I first learned to drive a car, it was a harrowing experience. I took ten weeks of lessons at a driving school, which were very helpful. But it was not until I was preparing for my road test that I found out how inexperienced I really was. That was really the problem. In my last trial run, I backed the car our of my driveway and hit a lamppost, but it was not badly damaged. That was only the beginning. I finally got the car moving smoothly, and was nervous about running into something else, but I didn't let it show. I was cruising along at 40 kilometres per hour with the radio playing, which always helped to calm me down. A police officer who was patrolling the neighbourhood must have thought I was going too slowly and pulled me over! We talked for a few minutes, and it turned out to be rather helpful; he suggested I use the headlights while driving at night.

<u>B</u>. When I was informed about the rally, it was an exciting event. As soon as I heard about the demonstration, I got them ready. They had shiny leather tops, brand-new laces, and thick rubber soles, which put me in the right frame of mind for walking. I really believed in the cause, which was why I looked forward to the march with great anticipation. Sometimes I get weary during a long walk, but I never let it show. Besides, this was a truly important demonstration. When I slid my feet into my shoes, this time they did not ache at all.

<u>C</u>. The Dolly Parton, nine-to-five workday, which millions of people experience five times a week, may be slowly dying out, which would make many people truly happy. Employers are telling their employees that they could use some extra time to themselves. A four-day workweek may be with us shortly, and they are pleased to have the chance to spend more time with their families. Fathers and mothers will be able to take up new hobbies and pursue new interests, and it will serve to improve the health of many people. This applies to both physical and mental health. Working fewer hours would make millions of people extremely happy, but it would have to go along with a promise of no drop in income. There are still some problems in setting up the shortened working schedule, but they are confident that as the need for it becomes more apparent, it will come about.

Part 6: Faulty Parallelism

Revise each sentence containing faulty parallelism.

<u>A</u>. A library is a good place to spend an afternoon and relaxing. You can read the newspaper from any major city, spend time looking for a good novel, or listening to a record. Librarians can tell you where to find a particular book and a quiet place to read it. Many libraries have display halls where you can observe artwork or just strolling around.

<u>B</u>. People find many different things to do in the library. There is usually

The Careful Eye

someone studying or write a research paper; there are those who read periodicals and those just chatting with a friend. All things considered, the library is an excellent place for meeting people to read, or to relax.

<u>C</u>. When we heard that we had won the lottery, we wanted to jump for joy, scream our lungs out, and patting each other on the back. We immediately made plans for a car that we could rent, dining, and dancing. We went wild, spending the evening eating the best food we had ever tasted, drinking only the finest wines, and we rode to the top of the CN Tower to get a dramatic view of Toronto by night. Finally, around 3 a.m. we decided that we were pooped, that we had to go home, and we wanted to climb into bed.

<u>D</u>. Paul Newman is one of today's most popular actors. Not only is he a big drawing card, he also has a lot of talent. He has played in many pictures including <u>The Hustler</u> and <u>The Sting</u>, and starring most of the time. We used to see him undressing, but now he dresses. Many women feel he is handsome and has sex appeal; he appears to be tough and have a strong will to many men.

<u>E</u>. In <u>Butch Cassidy and the Sundance Kid</u> he appeared with Robert Redford, another extremely popular actor. In that movie, they robbed banks, diving off a steep cliff, and to live with a beautiful woman who

was played by Katherine Ross.

F. Paul Newman lives with his wife, Joanne Woodward, in Connecticut. They live in a beautiful town, sharing a lovely house, and that the rumour is they have a genuinely happy marriage.

Part 7: Number, Person, Tense

Revise these three passages correcting all needless shifts in number, person, and tense.

A. If one intends to be a writer, you must first learn the great task of self-discipline. Most novelists or poets or dramatists do not work in an office; he often works at home. If he is unable to rid himself of distractions, they will probably find that they do very little work. There are always plenty of reasons or excuses not to write, but if the writer is able to set his mind to their work, he will not bother them. Some writers make schedules for themselves; others choose to work when they are inspired. Whatever the case, the point remained the same: if one wants to write, you write: if one does not, you don't.

B. Today, news programs and magazines were quite the rage. Everywhere you look, I can see news of this strike or that tax increase thrown at you. A newspaper should be objective, but they always seem to inject their own opinion into the stories. Because of the subjective nature of

The Careful Eye

the news, more and more magazines find its way onto the newsstands. Moreover, these magazines often produced more in-depth accounts of the news. I suppose every form of the news media has their place.

C. I work in a bank, and when you have that type of job, you have to be willing to wake up at a very early hour. I drive to work, park my car, and walked a block to work. I get a lunchbreak every day at noon, and they love to eat at the delicatessen around the corner. I worked at the bank for over a year, and decided that I had had enough. After looking around for a new job, I found one where you had to be at work by 6 a.m. This job was in a restaurant where you had to stand up all day, and after six months, I decided to go back to the bank. The manager was very nice to me and says, "You can have your old job back if one promises to stay at least two years." I take the job, and I enjoyed an extra hour of sleep every morning.

Part 8: Question marks, exclamation points, quotation marks, periods

Revise these two sections. Correct by using the punctuation noted in the title.

A. "This is the third paper of the semester that you have turned in late said Professor Martin and you are simply going to have to change your work habits." I know said Bruce, and I promise to change my ways. "I don't have a dog, replied Bruce, but I do have a little brother. "And he tore it up? Ms. Martin queried.""No, said Bruce," but he wrote it for me, and since his spelling was so bad, it took me two whole days to correct it."

B. Three men were stationed in the farthest reaches of northern Newfoundland, and their supply of whiskey was running low. Two of the men felt that they could take advantage of the third, so they told him to go out into the blizzard and buy some more whiskey in the nearest town. The third man said I will go only if you promise to save the last drop of this remaining whiskey for me. Don't worry the others said we promise. We promise, we promise, the others assured him. With that, the third man left. A day went by Two days went by A week and then two weeks went by. The two men figured that the third must have died in the blizzard and decided "to drink the last bit of whiskey." They took the bottle down from the shelf, and Cheers, and were about to indulge when the third man flung open the door. I told you I wasn't going if you drank the last drop. Newfie justice was served!

Part 9: Semicolons and colons

Proofread the following passages to correct all errors in semicolons and colons.

A. The team was in trouble: it had dropped from the first place to last in three weeks. The manager called a meeting of the players at which the following issues were discussed; the importance of developing a winning attitude, whereby the players would place the goals of the team over their individual achievements, the imposition of a strict curfew so that the players would be well rested for the games, the problem of teammates competing among themselves for higher salaries and greater coverage in the newspapers, and, last but not least, the general lack of hustle and determination on the part of the team's stars.

B. My friends and I recently spent a day driving near metro Toronto trying to hit as many hamburger joints as we could in 16 hours. Our travels took us to the following places; Burlington, where we prepared our stomachs with thick shakes and French fries, Concord, where we indulged in double bacon and cheese burgers, Hamilton, where we settled for soft drinks, Woodstock, where we each downed a filet of fish, and finally to Scarborough, where we celebrated with chicken sandwiches; we ate dessert at the quick lunch cafeteria at Trent University Peterborough ON.

Part 10: Commas

Correct all errors in the use of commas in these paragraphs.

A. We spent the day at my grandmother's cottage, on the beach, we had a great time. My wife and I, together with two friends, drove about sixty miles, from our home to the small two-bedroom beach house which had been built over a hundred years ago. We stopped at a small market, to pick up some food, for sandwiches, and ate as soon as we arrived at the cottage. We spent the rest of the day, eating drinking sunning ourselves going for walks and swimming. By the time the sun went down we were thoroughly exhausted. Isn't it strange I ask you that doing nothing can make you so tired?

B. Liberal Arts contrary to what some people think provides a good basis for an education. It is important I believe for every student to be well grounded in such subjects as Art History Science, Politics and English. These subjects give students a good idea, of what has been accomplished in the history of the world, and what is yet to be accomplished. By the time one completes a full program in Liberal Arts he/she will be ready to live with vigour, and vitality.

Part 11: Apostrophes

Correct these two passages by eliminating all errors in possessives and contractions.

A. Ella Fitzgeralds style of singing is one of the most exciting I ever heard. Without any formal training in music, shes managed to develop her voice to it's full potential. Whose ever going to dispute the statement that her scat singing makes her voice sound like a musical instrument? Ellas versions of Cole Porters songs are particularly moving and beautiful. S/He is able to understand the songs so well, and get so much feeling into Porters lyric's that listening to her performances becomes one of lifes great pleasures.

B. Ive never been one to keep New Years resolutions. Its always been easy enough for me to promise to give up mine bad habits, but I just dont seem to keep my promises. Once, the day after Id resolved never to smoke cigarettes again, my wife found a pack around and yelled, "Who's are these?" "Their mine," I answered sheepishly. Its a sure bet Ill resolve to quite again this year, but unless I get serious, Im sure my wifes advice that "Your never serious about something until your serious about it" will once again prove true.

Part 12: Apostrophes

Correct all incorrect uses of plurals and possessives within this article. Put your correction neatly above the error.

Randy and Elizabeth's Cottage

Yesterday's weather appeared quite promising as we set out for Randy and Elizabeths cottage. We decided on the spur of the moment to take along our neighbours children, even though they had previous arrangements' to play with their next-door neighbour's children, the Field's. Randy's and Elizabeth's cottage sit's in an idyllic garden with other cottage's near Parry Sound. They have an exquisite view of the Sound, especially the birds', the boat's, and the sunsets. Its a pleasant drive from North York and it feels good to escape from the cities hectic hustle.

Randy is an accountant in two northern rural Bank Branches, so we frequently tease him about where he gets his money. He insist's its the money from his father-in-laws' estate. But we know his father-in-law teache's at Humber Colleges Lakeshore Campus. Our arrival at Randy and Elizabeths cottage was delayed because our neighbours young pups tail got caught in the car door. The neighbour's were afraid it was broken, so we drove them from one Animal Clinic to another looking for one that was open after 8 p.m. on Friday night's. The veterinarian assured us Springs tail was not broken, but billed us $84.75 all the same. For three minutes work! Our neighbours youngest boy asked if the cost was covered by OHIPs current guidelines. Our neighbours' think their dog is family. Had we known there were three clinic's near Randy and Elizabeth, we could have gone to Elizabeths doctors office by motorboat.

Part 13: Plurals and Possessives

Correct this paragraph for plurals, possessives, and spelling

The Zabans

One of the Zabans interprises went under yesterday, so Mr. Zaban said. The families lawyers' made a brief statement today that the Abdool Zabans' will take complete control of the empire. It was found that Mr.

The Careful Eye

Zaban was allowing the managers wive's to use company expence acounts' for personnel reason's. All the other interprisers books are now under investigation's by Abdool. He suspects the accountants entries hide many fraud's in the book's. Many of the books pages were missing. He asked the policemens accountant if this was ellegal and he said it can be. Abdool then questioned weather the police investigators reports included this and if they suspect he was uninvolved. He then asked if the reporters reports will tell of his innocents. He finally left takeing all exciting secretaries notes. Zabans daughter, Sheena, as well as her husband Daryl, does'nt know what the future of her fathers' business will be.

Punctuation, Pronouns

Proofread this review for punctuation and pronouns

This is Spinal Tap

What should one do if he/she wants to learn more about the exotic, highminded, altruistic life of a rock star? Well, one could pour over the numerous articles, interviews, biographies, and diaries of such people, or one could go to his/her local video store and rent <u>This is Spinal Tap</u> directed by Bob Reiner and starring Christopher Guest.

<u>This is Spinal Tap</u> is a documentary (or "rockumentary", if you will) about fictional English rockers, Spinal Top. The film outlines their rise to stardom and follows the release and subsequent tour of their latest lp. <u>Smell the Glove</u> . As the camera travels with the band, the viewer gets an inside look at the trials and tribulations of touring, life on the road, and the general rock and roll lifestyle.

This includes the band's transition although various styles (pop, folk, heavy metal), the staggering array of drummers the band has employed, the management problems, concert cancellations, record company hassles and classic band breakup because of a tampering girlfriend.

The interviews, concert footage, and candid shots serve to portray the typical rock band stereotype: four or five middle aged men generally obsessed with sex, drugs and rock and roll, although in the words of immortal drummer Mick Shrimpton "as long as there are sex and drugs, I could probably do without the rock and roll."

The film is incredibly successful in that it is able to portray so many common situations familiar to playing musicians. Be it the failure of equipment or wrong bookings, Reiner has made an extremely insightful film as to the realities and misconceptions of the rock musician and his role in society. In so doing, Reiner may have made the film somewhat inaccessible to those outside the field, and may in fact leave the average viewer in the dark. Some of the best lines in the movie may evoke an "I don't get it" from a mainstream audience. This does not, however, alter the brilliant writing and acting in the film, but only confirms that it was not intended as a mainstream blockbuster. In fact, <u>Spinal Tap</u> has earned its place as a cult movie classic.

Band documentaries are nothing new. There are almost certainly as many movies about bands as there are bands themselves, and indeed parodies of documentaries (such as Eric Edle's <u>The Ruttles</u>) are fairly commonplace as well. <u>Spinal Tap</u> stands out among these however, as it presents more of a musician's view of musicians.

The involvement of Christopher Guest in the writing of the screenplay, allows the humour to "ring true" in a way an "outsider" could never achieve. Indeed as young musicians become more experienced in the field, their appreciation of certain scenes will almost certainly be heightened. Reiner left almost no stone unturned, and makes light of almost every stumbling block and glitch that all musicians face at one time or another. <u>Spinal Tap</u> is a definitive satire; it creates humour through the presentation of realistic elements, and gives us a tongue-in-cheek look at the lifestyle of that most peculiar being: the modern rock musician!

The Careful Eye

Fragments

Edit the following letter to correct all errors, especially fragments.

Dear Customer,

All of our customers have two things in common:

They insist on dressing upscale. And they insist on paying downscale.

And that's just the way we want it.

Because this is the season when the expensive menswear stores blare their trumpets and reduce their prices. On last season's leftovers. Everything they spent all spring trying to sell you . . . and couldn't.

Which is a perfect opportuniy to remind you that everything at our store is sold at those expensive stores. Everything. Always.

But everything here is always discounted 30% to 50%. Not the leftovers. Everything. Always.

And that includes our brand-new shipment of suits and blazers tailored on the finest Italian Super 100's High Twist wools. In the most sought after colours: rich blue, grey and olive. And our just arrived pure cotton white shirts . . . in either broadcloth or Sea Island Cotton.

Sure the expensive stores are offering reduced prices on "selected" items.

The difference is here you do the selecting.

Sincerely,

Tigran Petrosian
Manager

P.S. A reminder for Father's Day on June 9th, 3 Italian silk ties for $60.

142

Section III
Editing and Proofreading
Level II

The Careful Eye

Sentence variety, diction

1. Edit the following article for sentence variety, coherence, and professional tone.

2. Proofread for all errors in grammar, spelling, punctuation, and word choice.

On-the-Job Performance

Life consists of many experiences that very often cause an individual to extend beyond proper limits. During my life, I have encountered very many experiences but by living through these experiences I gained very practical knowledge, wisdom, and skills that prepared me to live in any society. Emmigrating to Canada is one experience that would linger in my memory for a very long time. During my first few months in Canada, I had to undergo many disappointments and failures before experiencing success.

Choosing a career was a very difficult task: it meant finding the right job to suite my academic qualifications, and to consider going back to school. My first job as a receptionist at K. Klintock & Co. (Canada) Ltd. was a memorable one. My faith, patience, and ability were tested. Some of the staff members were unscropulous, and devised plans that would have led to my dismissal. Fortunately, after my three month probation period I was hired permanent. Six months later I was promoted to to the Accounting Department as a junior clerk. My job became more complicated, one aspect was data entry and that required the use of a computer, which at that time was a novelty to me. I did experience some difficulty trying to learn the mechanical layout of both the printer and the computer.

Within six months, two receptionist were hired and dismissed. Finding an efficient person was a problem, so I was asked to take control of the switch board. I refused the offer; I felt cheated. And thought that I should be given a fair chance to improve my abilities.

Two weeks later, our accounting head office in New York decided to change the old computer system; therefore, I had to attend a one day training program at our New York office. On the day of the seminar, after a spagheti lunch I could not stay awake. I dozed off, and did not fully participate for the remainder of the seminar. Late that evening, I returned to Toronto. The following day the new computer system was installed in my office. I had problems then trying to operate the system, and in the mean time my boss pressured me to return to the switch board.

It was at the end of the spring semester, and I had to write my final examinations for the two courses I had been studying at Humber College. After that was over, I had enough time to review my situation.

I scaned through a dozen operator's manuals, hoping to acquire some answers to my questions.

Finallly, I decided to use a trial and error method which worked to a point. Nevertheless, after one month of seirous work I was able to master the new computer system. In addition, I was also succesful with my two courses.

The Careful Eye

Hyphens, Commas

> Proofread the following article for punctuation, paying particular attention to hyphens and commas.

Mrs. Grabbenclutch

Someone is striding through the steel-grey shaded corridors of the new Humber Library. In the doorway, a middle-aged figure appears. She wears a tailored off-white suit turquoise blouse with complementary jewellery — turquoise and silver pin, and silver and pearl ring and a multicoloured scarf in orange, turquoise, and off-white bowed deftly below her little second chin. Moving in low-heeled shoes of the "wrong" red. She clomps down the marbled ramp heel first bearing a weight that makes her legs resemble a dachshounds'. She carries too much. The high heels of former days now merely wag behind in a kind of independent existence, useful only for peer - pressured, younger teenage daughters who have temporarily deserted her and who as she articulates have left her with an empty nest. Her well groomed hair is red like a Chou's bushy red; her freckles fresh and big; her lipstick orange. The image is fleeting but familiar.

My alarm vanishes nonetheless. This resolute figure is neither a gangly teenager dressed in her mother's clothing of the sixties nor the wicked witch from Hansel and Grethel. No. Is she someone I know? Dazzling and shining eyes reveal character only somewhat disguised by the dramatic expression of casual "get-up". The child radiates from this carefree, make-believe adult who, while on her way to class would rather play with her favourite toy, an off-

The Careful Eye

white Volkswagen convertible, affectionately known as "Bugg". She realizes that toys are an extension of a child's resources for dramatic play, so to perpetuate the dramatic effect she pretends that little "Bugg" must be put to bed before dusk. But what can be said of Mrs. Grabbenclutch's continually carrying so many plastic bags!

Verbals

> Convert the underlined words in the following article to a participial, infinitive, or gerund phrase. Make all additional changes to punctuation and sentence structure where dictated by these changes.

Chivalry Is Dead

To be perfectly frank, my car is reliable. It runs most of the time, and gets me from here to there most of the time. Because my friend was looking for a new convertible, I offered to take my car on our shopping spree. <u>I met</u> her at her house, and gentlemanly walked to the passenger side of the car, opened the door, and, immediately <u>announced</u> that chivalry was dead, stepped in front of her and climbed into the front seat of the car while she stood there dumbfounded at my most uncharacteristic behaviour. When I explained that my two-door automobile had been reclassified as a one-door jalopy, she looked surprised, but <u>accepted</u> my explanation.

Then I mentioned that since it was raining, we'd need an umbrella or two. She agreed, already <u>noticing</u> two lying on the back seat. What she didn't understand was that we'd need umbrellas "in" the car: that was surprise number two. Rust had eaten through the roof above the windshield on the passenger's side of my car. Even commercial Goop was no longer effective, although it was guaranteed to mend just about everything; it had long since replaced kleenex. The hole was annoyingly large and the rain trickled inside the window frame <u>finding</u> a convenient, natural viaduct first on the door handle, and later on the right calf of my

The Careful Eye

passenger, who was startled, and was now amused. Neither was the driver's side of the car immune to inclemency, for the door, fixed as it is, had rusted in its position with one inch of sky visible between the top of the door and the door frame itself. I <u>was aware</u> of this phenomenon, and I kept abreast of daily, local weather forecasts and pointedly parked my car so that the prevailing wind and rain would blow on the passenger's side rather than on the driver's side. To increase the probability of a dry seat for the driver was the intent. This time I <u>achieved</u> momentary success.

<u>As I drive</u> into the rain, I inevitably had to sit knockkneed keeping my left leg away from the Chevy waterfall. If the wind did not blow rain in the gap between the window and its frame, the directional turns effected the same result. The water fell miraculously between the door and me. It always missed this door handle, formerly recessed, but now perpendicular to the door and bearing a cardboard sign: "Thanks, I know!" My curious passenger <u>succumbed</u> to politeness and let this incident pass sans comment. Could we possible be sitting in a twenty-first century Noah's ark? We could have been except for two sizeable holes in the floor beneath the carpet which provided natural, efficient drainage. Out feet stayed dry. I ingeniously discovered, some time earlier, that winter-weight floor mats used year round on top of the carpet prevent an up-to-date Fred and Wilma Flintstone characterization for my wife and me. Today, my friend and I were saved too. There were no plugged drains!

"Have you ever been seasick?" I queried.

"No, why do you ask?" she responded quizzically.

"Watch the hood of my car!" I counter-charged jocularly, realizing its apparent unsafety. (It oscillated about 30 degrees between the forces of the wind and the acceleration.)

The spring in this hood <u>wore out</u> months ago, and combined with the unevenness of the streets, caused the hood to flop haphazardly as if suspended between its normal positions: locked and open. It was an unnerving situation for my first-time passenger. <u>I knew</u> this latch was secure, so I exploited her ignorance, ignored her concerns, and teased her about riding in my convertible!

I developed a strategy to deal with stop-light situations which I had come to dread over the last few months, dread not so much because of the faulty brakes for they were mechanically sound — Midas said so — but because of other drivers' comments. Some responsibly <u>indicated</u> that my driver's door was open, and pointed with their index fingers. I read their lips: "O-pen".

"No, not open," I'd reply with the occasional success.

Winter salt on the 401 over the last decade won the battle with Ziebart and left the door permanently ajar, but not "open". In its stationary position, it

The Careful Eye

too was unnaturally "safe".

Less courteous drivers <u>gesticulated</u> vigorously and pointed to my door suggesting that I should shut it. If they did so kindly, I responded politely. For those who took it upon themselves to be obstinate, self-righteous, and lippy, I needed a solution that even kindness itself could not touch. I had tried. It didn't work. To quell the barbs of those unkind ones, I manoeuvred without ever looking in their direction a second time. I <u>calmly held up</u> my cardboard, handwritten sign that, to the courteous said, "Thanks, I know!" to the others read: "Picking your nose does become you." I made my point efficiently; my friend never witnessed that side of the sign.

She later bought her car. Now we occasionally park side by side in the college parking lot — her Mediterranean blue and silver Carrera 4 beside my green and rust Chevrolet Citation. They're both convertible, but with two more payments I'll own mine.

The Careful Eye

Spelling, Diction, Fragments

> Proofread the following review of Death Trap for errors in spelling, word choice, and fragments.

Death Trap I

Deathtrap, a movie by Jay P. Allen, is a sneaky who-dun-it based on a play by Ira Levin. Michael Caine, Christopher Reeve, and Dyan Cannon play the three main pieces of this puzzle. Which is full of twists and surprises. For the most part, the action takes place at an isolated, eccentric old house on Long Island. Sydney Bruhl (Mr. Caine), although a well-known mystery play writer, has just released his latest work in a long run of stinkers. Sheer coincidence would have it that on the disasterous opening night, Sidney is sent a copy of a play. Recently written by a former student (Mr. Reeve). Sydney, realizing immediately that the play will be a monsters hit and in desperate need of one himself, would do anything to have the play to call his own. Under the guise of providing expert experience to the final draft, Sydney and his slightly bubbleheaded wife (Dyan Cannon) invite the young writer to their house. They are care full to ensure that the only copy of the script be brought along as well.

The direction is clever, and although the movie is suspense full, it is not of the edge-of-your-seat variety. The choice of location, actually an old converted windmill, is stylish. And kind of creepy. It is a very believable setting for Sydney and Myra. Complete with an eccentric, nutty neighbor—Helga Ten Dorp—played very well by Irene Worth. There are

153

plenty of rich, kooky people living on Long Island.

All of the characters are portrayed very well in this feature. Dyan Cannon was an excellent casting choice for the role of the dizzy, high-strung Myra Bruhl. Chris Reeve, known to many as Superman, turns in an equally impressive performance. For Michael Caine, the obvious comparison is to his role in the movie <u>Sleath</u>. Mr. Caine brings a dry, sneaky ness to his character. That at times can be quite comical.

All in all, "<u>Deathtrap</u>" is an entertaining feature. The fact however, is that the story line becomes so bizzare at times it would be very unbelievable if not for the strong performances of the cast. The light humor is effective when combined with this type of mystery plot, and adds to the enviroment created by Tony Waton and Jay P. Allan.

Fragments, Wrong words, Spelling

1. Proofread this review of Death Trap for fragments, misspellings, wrong words, and punctuation. Make all corrections neatly above the errors.

2. Edit the review for consistency in person, professionalism in tone, and copy your version on a separate sheet of paper.

Death Trap II

Death Trap - Based on the novel by Ira Leven.

A very appropriate title for this movie since, from start to finish. It is a deathtrap.

The producer (Tony Waton) of DeathTrap portrays life to the viewer as sometimes very complex and hard to understand, where one minute you may believe something and yet you will never really know the truth until it is too late. As Dyan Cannon-Mira Bruhl (a playwright's wife) had lived through. The producer uses a subject of irony throughout the entire movie, one thing after the next leading into a pot full of laughter and irony.

After viewing the movie one can sit back and just laugh about it. The supporting actors Irene Worth (playing Helga Tendorp) and Henry Jones (playing Porter Milbred) were very strong. Helga Tendorp a european sycic adds a little flavour to the movie, always adding a pile of humour, with her humourous ways of communicating with her neighbours Mira Bruhl, Sydney Bruhl (the famous playwright) acted by Michael Caine. One must not forget the young homosexual student Clifford Anderson played by Christopher Reeve, adds another flavour to our mixed bowl of fruits.

The film always seems to keep the interest of the viewer, mainly because of its unexpected events one after another. The plot starts on one side of the fence and goes straight to the other side.

One must also complement the musical score. The music gives great expression where it is needed building tension at the correct moment. One must say that the strongest points of Deathtrap are it unexpecting events and its music.

A little about the film:

Being very ironic that the playwright who is down in the dumps all of a sudden receives a play in the mail written by a student of his, and the play is a masterpiece one can't see anything too fishy about this except that Sydney Bruhl wants to kill his student for the play, and it just so happens that he has only two copies of this play. Now it is getting a little unusual, to add to these parts who else should walk in but the lady of weirdness, Helga Tendorp she is a sycic and predicts the future consistently, a little ususual yet everything goes as planned and eventually we find out that our famous playwright is a homosexual (totally bizarre) catching everyone off guard what will they think of next. As the film goes on it just gets juicier. Tables seem to turn left and right one can never predict what will happen next, unless you named Helga Tendorp. At the end of the film one can even wonder if Helga Tendorp predicted her future this question is left with the viewer.

Overall the film Deathtrap is a great success, it is very humourous and creative. A film I recommend watching if you are into that "Who Done it?" motif. I would rate it an 8.5 out of 10.

The Careful Eye

Mechanics, Spelling, Punctuation

Proofread the review of Death Trap for all errors in grammar, mechanics, spelling, and punctuation.

Death Trap III

Death Trap staring Michael Caine and Christopher Reeves is an entartaining, cleverly written and tastefully directed film that keeps the audience on the edge of there seats and satirizes the typical murder mystery.

The film is about a successful playwright who plots to kill his wife with his homo-sexual lover who wants to write the events down for a play. Michael Caine's character is very disturbed about this because this play holds evidence that could very well incriminate him of the murder, so he tries to kill his companion before he can finish the play. From the minute the audience is aware of the deception between the two main characters there is an exciting ora of tension which was created by director. He did this by using excellent camera shots and tension building music. Another factor in creating this tension were the facial expressions of the two leads. Michael Caine was particularly good at this and he expertise at this type of role is evident throughout this film as it was not as satirical.

The movie Deathtrap is a satire of the typical murder mystery in the way that it uses a lot of cleches for humor and for the corny yet classic feeling of true play of this nature. An example of this occurs when Christopher Reeves is holding Michael Caine at gun point and he makes note of the thunder and lightening out side calling it "a bit corny but effective." The plot itself is rather tough and cheek in the way that the surprising turn of events were made light of by the excellent acting and sutlily sarcastic music and screenplay. The set of the movie was very much like a stage set in the way that from every angle you could see the entire room. The weapons were conveniently placed in te picture almost all of the time to keep the audience aware of the tense and frightening atmosphere.

One of the strongest points of this film is the clumsy playwright trying to be a brilliant killer and the slightly mysterious apprentice who we learn is a mentally disturbed person. These two characteristics are perfect and to top it off they are alone at a country house far from anyone who could suspect anything. For the exception of one person who keeps intruding into there lives. This is none other than the suspicious psychic with the eery German accent that lives close by and keeps dropping in unexpectedly to solve the crime, But she consistently and hunourously gets her feelings mixed up and comes up short. However she is resonable for creting a major part of the events to come in the movie.

This film is an excellent piece of work in all areas. It has a cleaver plot, along with well through out characters that were developed beutifully throughout the movie. The directing was outstanding as far as camera shots and tasteful execution of the script through the actors, and the actors did an excellent job creating just the right balance of tension and sarcasm to make this film a fun, exiting, thrilling, yet light movie. It dose what movies were suppose to do, entertain you. I'll give it and 8.5

The Careful Eye

Mixed punctuation, Diction

Proofread the following article for all errors in punctuation and word choice.

Proper Spelling — A Necessary Skill

The dictionary defines 'spelling' as the writing, correctly, all the letters of a word so as to make it explicit to the reader. If some of the spelling seen today is any indication more people ought to ponder the word 'correctly'.

Children learn to communicate through their writing and in the primary grades the emphasis is on the writing process, not on spelling accuracy. They're taught to put ideas down on paper using their own words in a rough draft. They than revise, edit and improve the content of what they have written so that the idea he or she wishes to express are clearly stated. Spelling be comes only a part of that editing or polishing process.

Some educators caution against an over-emphasis of correct spelling too early in the game. They think it inhibits a childs creative process and minimizes his or her willingness to explore different ways to express ideas, simply out of fear of making spelling errors. In many cases, that fear is clearly reflected in the unimaginative stilted writing that inevitably results.

Spelling should be taught in various ways including the discussion of words that appear in the children's books, school texts and other written material with which they are involved. But we moreover have to teach children the technical aspects of spelling and teach it across the whole curriculum, not just in a spelling or writting class. It is the unbalanced presentation of correct spelling that has caused all the trouble. As a consequence, we now have a generation or two of students (and exstudents) whom may have great imagination and lots of creative ideas, but whom are abysmal poor in spellin'. They have not grasped the fact, that correct spelling is a necesaary courtesy which enables the reader to follow the writers' thought process. The most visible component of the thoughts themselves.

If children remember words just for the sake of spelling tests they won't enjoy the challenge (and rewarts) of an expanded vocabulary for use in commuting with others but if they are taught daily, in every subject, the importance of good spelling, they will have a journey in, which good spelling, like good manners, will never let them down.

The Careful Eye

Tenses, Punctuation, Diction

Edit and proofread this review of This is Spinal Tap paying particular attention to tenses, punctuation, and diction.

Review of This Is Spinal Tap

This is Spinal Tap is a portrayal of the rise and fall of a fictional heavy metal band. Directed by Rob Reiner, it takes a humorous look at the bizarre world of rock music. Christopher Guest plays David St. Hubbins, the lead singer of Spinal Tap, as well as being a contributor to the script. Spinal Tap is done in the style of a documentary and follows the band on a come-back tour of America. It is an entertaining as well as insightful look into the life of a band on the road.

Interview footage and a video history of Spinal Tap is intermingled with tour and concert footage. We see the band at its humble beginnings in 1965 performing such classics as "Gimme Some Money" and "Listen to What the Flower People Say. The current tour begins in Philadelphia, then moves to Atlanta. There, the band learns that Polymer Records had rejected the album design for their newest release, "Smell the Glove". The cover shows a naked woman wearing a dog collar, down on all fours, being forced to sniff a black leather glove. However, the band cannot comprehend why this would be considered offensive or sexist.

From there on in, things only get worse for Spinal Tap. The show in Boston is cancelled, hotel reservations are screwed up, and David's wacko girlfriend flies in from London to join the band. Jeannie becomes manager for the band after an argument with Ian, the previous manager. She fancies herself to be something of an astrologer and draws up stat charts for the band. Finally, when she books Spinal Tap to play an 'at ease weekend' at an Air Force base, Nigel, the guitarist storms off stage and leaves the band. Spinal Tap truly hits rock bottom when they get second billing to a puppet show.

But, of course, there has to be a happy ending. Nigel reappears with the news from their former manager, Ian. 'Sex Farm' in on the charts in Japan. The band reforms and embarks on a Japanese tour.

This is Spinal Tap is a wonderful spoof of the rock 'n roll world. The characters are believable and well developed. Someone seeing this film without knowing that it is a comedy well might think that Spinal Tap is a real band. The script covers many aspects of life on the road. We see the band with a constantly changing cast of groupies. One particular scene demonstrates how the stress (and possible drug abuse) can take one to the breaking point. Nigel has a freakout about some catered food. The bread is too small, some olives are stuffed, some aren't. Really how can anyone be expected to cope with such ridiculous food?

Any rock musician who sees Spinal Tap will surely see the reality concealed beneath the comedy and nonsense. It is a vision of rock not far removed from the truth. Musicians, in the spotlight, are not always thoughtful visionaries, they are sometimes little more than children caught up in a wonderful game. But the game is too much for some. During the course of the film, Spinal Tap loses four drummers. One is killed in a bizarre gardening accident, another chokes on vomit, and two spontaneously combats. These fringe characters are based on the excapades and eventual demise of Keith Moon, drummer for The Who.

<u>Spinal Tap</u> is a triumph for Rob Reiner. He directs, stars, and shares a writing credit. Reiner extracts outstanding performances from all the actors involved. This film will never have a very wide audience appeal, but is destined to be a cult classic. Those who take the time to watch will watch again and again in sheer delight.

The Careful Eye

Punctuation, Spelling, Logic

1. Proofread this article for errors in punctuation, spelling, and word usage.
2. Edit the article for its illogical assumptions and its statements that are unsupported.
3. Copy your edited version on a separate sheet of paper.

Dangerous Dream World

I found your article in the Toronto Star, titled 'Teens live in dangerous dream world', quite thought provoking. While I do agree that these are difficult times for children to grow up in, and more so for teenagers, I don't think we can brand an entire generation of teenage boys as being reckless and irresponsible, and the girls as being star struck, hopeless romantics. Though I am not aware of the exact statistics, I do know that a large percentage of the teenagers today are more aware of what they face in their future than their parents were in their age.

The pressures exerted by society on teenagers today are indeed phenomenal, and make my teenage years blissfully tranquil in comparison. Things were different in those days; more straight forward and clearly defined. There were things a teenager did, that were socially acceptable, and others that weren't. Parents were respected, and conducted themselves in a manner that merited that respect. But with the advent of the '60's things changed. That generation of teenagers rebelled against the oppressiveness of the 'establishment'. "Flower power" and 'free love' became the dominant attitude of the time. Sex, drugs and rock music became the 'in' things, and thoughts of education and a career were temporarily shelved. These attitudes prevailed through the '70's and today's teenagers are products of that generation. So can we really blame them for what they are? They are what society has made them.

Things have changed quite radically in the '80's. Advances in technology, increases in population and the ups and downs of the economy have forced society to 'smarten up' and become more competitive than ever before. Today a teenager is conscious of the value of college education and painfully aware of the prospect of unemployment even after having attained one. Yes, certainly there are those who buckle under the stress and give up the fight, drop out of school and take to the streets, but at the same time, there are others who whilst enjoying themselves as teenagers will, are also striving very hard in our school and universities.

In this group, the girls and boys seem to have the same priorities as far as self development is concerned. We have more women in the work force today than ever before, and they aren't all working as seamstresses in a factory or as waitresses, nurses, typists and secretaries either. Gone are the days when there were clear lines drawn between women's jobs and men's jobs. Today we have some women in the poisitions ranging from prime minister to auto mechanic; corporate executive to construction worker; computer scientist to astronaut. This range is most definitely not shrinking, as is evident from the enrollment statistics at our universities. Most teenage girls are competing shoulder to shoulder with their male counterparts, venturing into fields that either did not exist or were not open to their predecessors. Girls are definitely more career conscius today and statistics do show that they aren't as eager to be tied down to the responsibilities of marriage and motherhood until the have established themselves.

Sure, teenagers today do have their problems; just as we did, and our parents before us. The nature and volume of these problems has changed, but teenagers are a tough and resilient bunch and though some do get derailed along the way, the majority will bounce back on track and get on with the rest of their lives.

Agreement, Tenses, Punctuation

Proofread the following article correcting agreement, tenses, and punctuation.

Guitar Concerto

The Guitar is an intimate instrument where the listener should be about ten-feet from the performer. There is often a collision of the guitar's intimacy and the largeness of the Concert Hall, the intimate sounds of the guitar draw one closer to the performer, while the loud sounds of the Orchestra can and do force one back, away from the source.

R. Murray Schafer tries to balance the orchestra and the guitar, but he tries to have the balance devoid of anything inimical (hostile). The orchestra must speak, but the tradition was for the guitar to speak and then for the orchestra to repeat what the guitar said; this is not what Schafer does in this new composition: Guitar Concerto. He stresses the bonding of the two.

Norbert Craft, the Guitarist, suggested that Schafer include percussion as part of the orchestration and Schafer agrees.
Some of the special, percussive effects include a musical, saw played by synthesizer, a spoon, tapped on the guitar, and bending, strings to get quarter tones, but this was done on violins, not on the guitar.

In the final portion of the composition, there is a definite middle eastern flair with the use of the "ud" (Schafer's favourite instrument, and the "daribuka", a middle eastern Drum.)

Schafer maintains that the toughest job is to bond the orchestra and the guitar together rather than follow the original often-played scenario of statement and repetition of statement.

The debut aired on Sunday April 8, 1990 on FM 1010 at 9.05.

The Careful Eye

Punctuation, Word choice, Person shifts

1. Proofread this article for errors in word choice, punctuation, and person consistency.

2. Edit the article to make it unified and coherent through a variety of sentence patterns. Think of the final effect that should be both flowing and concise.

Tough and Athletic

I once had a teacher in high school, who was one of the toughest gym teachers, in the school. She was not only tough, but she was also an athlete. She thought just because she ran fifteen miles a day, that her class should also, run fifteen miles a day. After, one of her classes you were so physically tired you didn't want to spend the rest of the day at school. You see, this was the first and last class of the day, for most students. I had no other alternatives, but to accepted this challenge, and what a challenge it was. It's funny though, she was the only gym teacher who ran with his or her gym class. She had muscles on top of muscles, and I guess she thought, we might won't be as fit as herself, however, I'm sure she is more fir then I'll ever be. The teacher would start the class off by running a mile or two miles, around the park. Some of my friends, and I would take short cuts or take our time running. She hated us , when we took to long. We would usually end up returning after school or running around the park again. After, the run the class would go back into the gym for more physical pain. Push up, sit ups, leg stretches, jumping jacks, and everything else she wanted to do. The class would then, play a sport. The game wouldn't last to long, because, we spent most of our time working our for the merrathon.

I know she was a good teacher; although, she could have been a little easyer on us. Her life revolved around exercise, and keeping fit, mine, however, didn't. I would of liked to spend most of gym time playing sports. Because, you're having fun, and you don't get as tired, as you would, if you were doing sit-ups most of the time. After the year of trying to make me an athlete had passed, I wouldn't ever consider taking another gym class because I didn't want to walk around in pain all of the time. Every muscle in my body, would be over worked. I had pain on top of pain instead, of, muscle on top of muscle. You could say I had avoided the challenge the next year.

The Careful Eye

Style, Editing

1. Proofread the following paragraph.

2. Keeping the same general ideas, edit and rewrite this paragraph to elevate both the style and the diction and correct all grammatical errors.

A Qualified Secretary

A qualified secretary should have three basic secretarial skills. First, she should have fast and accurate typing, so that she could complete her daily tasks. This will give her the abilities to present her work in an organized fashion. Also, she should have a good communication skill, in order to give clear and concise information to her boss, or to her companies customers and employees. Having this will enable her to improve herself as an individual. Finally, proper english is a plus when addressing a solution to a problem. It can give the other individual a clear understanding of what you are trying to say. With these secretarial skills, she will develop herself as a qualified Secretary.

The Careful Eye

Verbs, Agreement, Fragments, Comma splices, Logic

Correct the following paragrahs paying specific attention to verbs and verb tenses, pronoun antecedent and subject-verb agreement, fragments and comma splices, and, especially in paragraph three, logic.

Cars and Personalities

Automobiles often reflects the personalities and financial status of their owners. The class of people range from lower, middle, upper middle, and, finally, the rich.

We usually associated lower income earners with blue collar jobs. Their education is limited and chances for advancement are quit slim. Quite simply put, means they would be fairly hard prest to become a higher income earner. They would be fairly easy to indentify in a crowd. Not as well dressed and mannerisms that are not as refined as a higher income earner. Their automobiles are predictable five to ten years old, and certainly not stylish.

Their is a split with middle class earners, some are blue collar and others hold low end white collar jobs. Plumbers, electrician, and carpenters are a few examples of higher paying blue collar jobs. Low end white collar jobs are assisting the manager or perhaps a clerk in an office. With more education than the lower class, these people have better communication skills that clearly sets them apart from the lower class individuals. The automobiles which identify this class are usually one to five years old.

173

Domestic with few luxury options.

Sports cars and luxury autos come to mind when we think of the upper middle class. Clearly more educated than there counterparts. College or university degrees are the norm for this group. Upper management is a typical place to find these income earners. Their education plays a major roll in determining their personality. Weather the topic be political, historical, or geographical they will always have a respected opinion. With an increase of income, comes an increase of socializing. This group likes to be seen in their Polos.

Mercedes Benz, B.M.W., Jaguar, names that relate to the rich and their lifestyle. University degrees are the norm at his level. They have outstanding abilities in regard to finance and are better know as the movers and shakers of the world. According to the lower classes, the rich are often viewed as snobbish and cold because of their hard-core business tactics. This maybe true, but it is the only way to survive in the corporate world.

There are acceptions to every rule, but for the most part the four classes of people describe hold true. Personality is a direct result of social status. If someone in a lower class moves to a higher class their personality will surely change. If you put all the different classes of people in one room wearing identical clothing it would not take long to identify the poor from the rich. The rich would present himself/herself in a more civilized way using a much higher level of vocabulary.

News Release

FOR IMMEDIATE RELEASE

Banks Found "Not Guilt"

Yet Receive Sentencing From

Commons Finance Committee

Vancouver, B.C. — During a speech earlier today, J.J. Quinn, senior vice-president british columbia and yukon individual bank CIBC defended bank service charges to a group of kiwanis club members regarding the recent report issued by the finance and economic affairs committee. 'It is as if the banks were charged, tried found not guilty and then sentenced', protested Quinn. The report proposes that the banks be required to offer free Basic Banking services.

The finance committee has charged the banks on three main issues outlined in their report. The committee stated that canadian banks have too high of service charges. That this was possibly due to third world debt, and that Banks were not fulfilling the bank acts' requirements. With their suggestions, the committee developed a private members bill which would force the banks to eliminate service charges.

In his defence, Quinn supported current charges by stating the improvements to customer services in recent years. Traditional banking hours have been supplanted by twenty-for hr. automatic banking machines. Interbranching banking has been improved, loans can not be attended in 24 hours and daily interest has also undergone improvements. "With this increase in service quality has come to a need to adjust the pricing regime', exclaimed Quinn. Instead of the burden falling on borrowers heads the user pay system was implemented so the cost of services offered will be share by all.

Regarding the use of funds from service charges towards loses from third World debt. "The committees' own research showed that it was wrong to link the two issues," pointed out Quinn. A comparison showed that the rate of service charges were simular to those of the trust companies and credit unions which do not carry the burden of Third World Debt.

Although no substantial evidence to convict the banks of not fulfilling the Bank Act's requirements, the committee persisted with a Private Member's Bill rather than the Government introducing legislation to the House of Commons. As Quinn outlined, "The role of a Parlamentary (sic.) Committee in this process is to examine appropriate issues and make recommendations to the Government regarding legislation. The committee has gone far outside of its mandate role as an advisory body and that private member's bills are just not supposed to be used that way." By introducing the Private Member's Bill, the banks lose all rights to control the rate of service charges.

An effort is being made to offer the best possible rate for the service being offered buy the banks and to communicate with effort to customers about service charges. "Some have all ready made significant changes to their pricing policies," Quinn expressed.

The Careful Eye

Word choice, Spelling, Agreement

Proofread the following article for accuracy in word choice, agreement, and spelling.

Impact of Language: Grammar and the Very Young

An English professor and his youngest of two daughters recently engaged in a bit of a dialog that suggest how furstrating grammer can be. The five-year old girl was accompanyed by a yonge friend when she ran up to his/her father and announced, "Daddy, me and Kathy wants some ice cream." The little girl waited several minutes while her father reads his newspaper. "You ought to have said 'Kathy and I'," was his curt reply. He consumed reading. Finally, in a genuine effort to express herself correct, she asked, "Daddy, are you going to buy some ice cream for Kathy and I?" The English professor put his newspaper aside and said, "Honey, you should have used Kathy and me". At that point the youngsters eyes' filled with gigantic tears' of frustration as she cried, "A few minutes ago you told me to use Kathy and I'.

The Careful Eye

Irregular verbs

In the following paragraph, correct all errors in the use of irregular verbs and commonly confused words.

Humouresque

Thursday was certainly not my day. As I set in my car to drove to Highland Farms, the ignition key brake and both peaces was soon laying on the floor mat. When I reached to bring them up, I hit my head on the stereo and the station changed. "A man was hung at dawn this morning in. . ." but that was all I herd. Misfortune staid with me throughout the day; in the Wordprocessing class, the professor was trying to learn me how to make columns. She demonstrated the process quickly on her IBM computer, and then I insisted, "Now, leave me do it!" I hit the cursor, lay my hands on my knees, and than set their waiting for columns too appear. Suddenly a power serge hit the computer centre. I rised my head and still seen nothing on the screen. Bev agreed I brung her to much trouble four won day and I should of stood in bed last Thursday!

Finally, when I tried two use the spell cheque too edit the preceding paragraph, their where know errors. Sew what is the point off having spell cheque, who's function is to catch Miss spellings, if, in the end, the errors go unnoticed? Its waist full to except technology as integral to hour education if we be come technologically illegitimate and functionally illiterate to.

The Careful Eye

Grammar, Diction, Punctuation

1. Proofread this address for grammar and punctuation.
2. Edit for appropriate diction, keeping in mind the nature of the address.

Valedictory Address I

Thank you students, parents, and faculty. It was three years and six tough semesters ago that I first began to attend classes here at Humber. During that time Ive alot of friends and learned quite a bit.

Being a music graduate I understand that I have a tough road ahead of me, but I know that Humber has prepared me for anything that I have to face. George Bernard Shaw once said "Hell is full of musical amateurs: music is the brandy of the damned." I see myself reflected in this quote as if I were standing at the fork in a road. I look down the left road and I can see that the road is very rocky and there are mud puddles, and broken glass scattered all over the road. As I open my eyes wider I see at the end of this old road a brand new sports car. Fully loaded! My eyes then wander to the right I see myself looking down the other road, this road, unlike the other one is paven throughout and has a slight decline to make it easy to walk down. However at the end of this road sits something a little different. Its like the sportscar is new, and it has four wheels, but it's a little red wagon. The wagon to me represents the easy way out.

I think most of us in life have to choices that we can make. They are the short easy white picket fence ones, or the long hard six car garage ones. Don't get me wrong though, but if there is one thing that every person in life should learn it is not to give up! Being at Humber has helped me realize this goal.

Now I know that I may not become a great musician, but I will never give up on my dream, and if there is one thing that everyone here can learn from me I hope it's the same that I learned from everyone here at Humber, students and teachers both! There is one thing I would like to ad, if I am not a successful musician I am going to be a success at something else, because I'm determined to get my six car garage! Thank you all for everything.

The Careful Eye

Pronoun agreement, Diction, Tenses

1. Proofread this address for pronoun agreement and tenses, and punctuation paying particular attention to the conditional.

2. Edit the address for diction, bearing in mind that it is a valedictorian address.

Valedictory Address II

Percy Bysshe Shelly once said, "Music, when soft voices die/ Vibrates the memory." After three short years here at Humber College Music Program, our minds and hearts are filled with memories of the dreams and hopes we envisioned and achieved, with the help of our friends and instructors. We learned, we applied what we learned through performance.

When I started at Humber in September of eighty-nine, like many others, I was so impressed by the dedicated teachers who were there not only to instruct, but give friendly advise and support. Musicians from every style and calibre joined the program, and it was so fascinating to see how these individuals with assertive, unique personalities meshed and blended. It didn't take long for groups of close friends to form. Lasting bonds were created and taken outside of school hours. Everyone kept their music style, but their friends always supported them. We've gave each other a piece of ourselves, a certain dance step, a certain groove, or that new guitar lick we've just stumbled into one day in a practise module. Theory got harder, ear training was nothing short of mind-boggling, and lead sheets were being written out every hour. Being a vocalist myself, I've really come to appreciate different voices, and what makes them cook. With the help and constant care that Trish Colter gave the vocalists, along with supportive critism and guidance Dave Stillwell provided, we were able to end off first year college with determination and belief that we will conquer second and third year with fyling colors.

I think the memories that stick out in our minds the most, shall have to be, the first performance in front of our peers. I'm sure we all stood there and thought, "Wait a minute, these aren't the idiotic tone deaf audiences I usually play for, and get away with murder because they don't know any better! These are musicians who'll know every note I messed up or missed out on!" But we've grown to care and love our peers, and in the end, provided something that the drunk tone-deaf audience couldn't—confidence and support, along with a wealth of knowledge from past experiences they've shared.

My friends have pulled me out of some scary experiences in the past three years. Getting up there and actually, seriously improvizing on chord changes, using all these crazy jazz lingo like "skoodie-oblee bop" was pretty devestating, let me tell you. Then you'd come home and tell your parents, boyfriend or girlfriend what you did this week, and they look at you funny and say "Are you sure about this career move dear?" There's nothing more amusing than to scat infrontof your conservative music-taste dad who thinks "La Boheme" is the greatest thing ever composed, and see the expression on

The Careful Eye

his face when you've completed. He obviously says, "They call THAT music? It doesn't even have a constant beat!" After three years, he's learned to put up with it. A matter of survival.

Now, after the grand recital we each performed, show casing all we've learned to the world, ready to take on life in the music industry, we leave behind us those textbooks, binders, small useless lockers that can hardly hold a suitcase. We leave behind the many wonderful teachers which have taught us so much along with the wisdom they've shown us. We say goodbye to many close friendships we've made which a written address and phone number on a piece of paper leaves the only link to some, and we say for many, goodbye to parents, siblings, boyfriends, and girlfriends, in order to fulfil that dream of being a "Big" performer, on Broadway, in a jazz club, on a film score, or on vinyl. But those soft voices of laughter, of cheers, and of that close friendly words you heard before you went on stage to give it your best, will always echo in your mind. And five, maybe ten years down the line, you'll be in an elevator, or a grocery store, or in your car listening to the radio, and you'll hear that familiar guitar lick, or that sweet tender voice you've heard before, or a title of a tune from the past, and you'll remember those college days where, now, here, is living proof that our dreams are one step away from reality through dedication, determination and a hunger for success. That's what they've taught at Humber College, and that's what we're going to do.

Teachers, parents, fellow friends, and all who've come out tonight to support these fine musicians, I wish you all the success in the world and I know truly that these memories will stay with me for time to come, as I know they will for you. Good luck to all, and a special thank you to everyone on the music faculty who've stuck by us. Lets keep in touch, and lets keep at it. See you under the spots!

The Careful Eye

Absolute modifiers, Adverbs, Correlative conjunctions

Proofread this address for the incorrect use of adverbs, absolute modifiers, and correlative conjunctions.

Valedictory Address III

When I enrolled in the music program three years ago, I was hoping to attain a level of playing proficiency which would enable me to perform at a competent, professional level. Having completed the program, I am able to say that through a lot of hard work, good instruction, performing situations and more hard work, I have achieved what I set out to do. But I have gained something else: experience and philosophies which have vastly enriched my outlook on music as a whole.

Shelley once wrote "We—are we not formed, as notes of music are. For one another, though dissimilar?" and coming to an understanding of this statement has been the single important aspect of my musical education. The music program introduced me to an enormous range of musical styles, and allowed me to experience through these styles many different cultures, traditions, and philosophies. I can remember Clarke Anderson in World Music class doing his very best to point out the merits of some extremely abstract, atonal, 20th century compositions. While some questioned the musical validity of such words, Clarke explained the process behind the piece and thus made it more accessible to the listner. Once, Brian Harris asked me to prepare a classic jazz ballod (Misty), for a private lesson.

Bored with the traditional manner of playing this piece, I embarked on a more adventurous interpretation; complete with boogie-woogie bass line and stride accompanyment. Far from being shocked, or dismayed, Brian complemented me on my imagination and daring, even though in the eyes of traditionalists, I destroyed the piece.

It is this type of approach which has helped me to appreciate the beauty and content of all styles, and has increased my appreciation for music as a whole.

Another intergral part of my education has been exposure to and interaction with other musicians. It is perhaps in this area that Shelley's words ring truest. I use to think that everyone generally heard things the way I did, but I have come to realize that music is experienced differently by everyone, and that everyone's emotional response is quite unique to any given piece of music. In playing with a variety of people I have come to see that a person's background, personality, and musical preference all converge to create something completely unique. Every musician has a slightly different angle on a piece of music, and thus something interesting and important to say about it. In any given classroom, there are 20 different musicians, therefore twenty truly unique statements, twenty outlooks, and most importantly twenty completely different teachers of musical philosophy: "For one another, though dissimilar".

The Careful Eye

Is Humber a good place to get your technique together? Yes. Is Humber a good place to learn to play jazz, and classical forms? Sure. It is all of these, but it's a lot more. Humber can be an important step in the creation of a musical career, a door to the whole universe of musical forms and outlooks, and can also be a part of the formation of a person as an individual. Humber has a lot of dissimilar notes enrolled in its program, but when they all come together, it's some of the sweetest harmony you'll ever hear.

Subject Index

GRAMMAR AND MECHANICS

AGREEMENT 72-74; 168-169; 178
A number 73
collective nouns 72
complements 74
compound subject 73
correlative conjunctions 24; 73
indefinite pronouns 72
measurement 73
money 73
neither and nor 73
only 74
or and nor 73
parts and portions 72
relative pronouns 20; 74
subject and verb 72
tenses 182-185
THE number 73
to be 74

CAPITALIZATION 175-177

CLAUSES 55-67; 90-92
complex 62-64
compound 59-61; 79-80
compound-complex 65-67
dependent 62; 65
independent 56; 62; 65
simple 56-58

COMMA SPLICES 75-78; 81-89

DICTION 153-154; 155-157;
160-161; 162-164; 172; 179;
180-181; 182-185

FRAGMENTS 114-115; 153-154;
155-157; 173-174

IRREGULAR VERBS 179

LOGIC 160-167; 196-197

MODIFIERS
absolute 186-188
dangling 126-127
misplaced 125-126

PARALLELISM 117-122; 129-131

PHRASES 55; 68-69; 90-92
absolute 38; 69
gerund 68
Infinitive 68
participal 68
prepositional 68
prepositional phrase included with subject 72

PERSON SHIFTS 100-101; 128-129; 131-132

PRONOUN ANTECEDENTS 98-99

PROOFREADING
(General editing) 123-138; 158-159; 160-161;
173-174; 180-181; 182-185; 186-188

RUN-ONS 76-78; 87-89; 116; 124

SENTENCES (also see clauses)
55-67; 107-112; 144-146

SPELLING
153-163; 165-167; 178

TENSES 26-30; 162-164; 168-169; 182-185
conditional mood 185-188
emphatic 30
future 26-28
past 26
present 26
future perfect 29
past perfect 29
present perfect 29
future progressive 30
past progressive 30
present progressive 23
progressive 30
shall and will 27-28
shifts 131-132
should 28

VERBALS 31-32; 102-106; 149-152
gerunds 16; 31; 102-106
infinitives 31; 102-106
participles 31; 102-106

PARTS OF SPEECH

ADJECTIVES 22; 31-32
complements 32
compound 47
participles 31
suspended compound 47

ADVERBS 23; 189-191
comparative 23
conjunctive 40
positive 23
superlative 23

CONJUNCTIONS 24; 81-86
co-ordinating 24; 37; 41
correlative 24; 73; 186-188
FAN BOYS 24; 37
subordinating 24

INTERJECTIONS 25; 38

NOUNS 15; 31
abstract 15
collective 16; 72
common 15
complements 32; 74
concrete 15
gerunds 16; 31
infinitives 31; 102-106
mass 16
proper 15

PREPOSITIONS 25
prepositional phrases 68
prepositional phrase included with subject 72

PRONOUNS 14; 20-21; 139-141; 128-129
antecedents 98-99
consistency 100-101; 170-171
demonstrative 20
indefinite 21; 72
interrogative 21
personal 20
reciprocal 21
reflexive 21
relative 17; 20; 74

VERBS 17
auxiliary 18
intransitive 17
irregular 179
linking 17
regular 18
strong 18-19
transitive 17

PUNCTUATION

APOSTROPHES 49-54; 93-95
contractions 50; 135-136
figures 51
its and it's (and its') 52-54
joint possession 51; 135-138
letters 51
omission 50-51
possession, plural 49-50; 135-138
possession, singular 49-50; 135-138
symbols 51
with personal pronouns 51

BRACKETS 44
quotations and 44
with sic 44

COLONS 42; 81-86
and semicolons 133-134
appositives 42
bibliography 42
chapters and verses 42
explanatory sentences 42
formal quotations 42
ratios 42
salutations 42
time 42
titles and subtitles 42

COMMAS 37-39; 81-89; 96-97; 147-148
absolute phrases 38
addresses 38; 39
Canadian use 37
confirmatory questions 39
contrast 39
co-ordinate adjectives 37
dates 39
direct address 38
FAN BOYS 24; 37
independent clauses 37
interjections 38
introductory dependent clauses 37; 39
names 38
omission of words 39
parenthetical expressions 38
preventing misreading 39
quotations 38

salutations 39; 42
series of words, phrases, clauses 37
yes and no 38

DASHES 43
attributing quotations 43
interruptions 43
parenthetical expressions 38; 43
summarizing statement 43

EXCLAMATION POINTS 36; 132-133

HYPHENS 47-48;
bibliography 48
compound adjectives 47; 144-146; 147-148
compound numbers 48
fractions 48
homonyms 47; 179
prefixes 47
suspended compound adjectives 47

ITALICS 46
books 46
magazines 46
newspapers 46
paintings 46
titles 46
underlining as substitute 46

PARENTHESES 45
deemphasis 45

PERIODS 33-35
abbreviations 33
American use 33
British use 33
Canadian use 33
commands 33
initials 33
nonsentences 34
numerals 33
omission 34
outlines 33
and quotation marks 35; 132-133
requests 33
statements 33

QUESTION MARKS 36; 132-133
commas and 36
direct questions 36
doubt 36

QUOTATION MARKS 44-45; 132-133
articles 45
chapters of books 45
definitions 45
direct quotations 44
lectures 45
poems 45
quotation marks and commas 38
single quotation marks 44
songs 45
titles 45
words used in special sense 44

SEMICOLONS 40-41; 81-86
and colons 130-134
conjunctive adverbs 40
co-ordinating conjunctions 41
independent clauses 40; 95-100
items in series with commas 41
lists of three or more 41

General Index

A
A number 73
abbreviations 33
absolute modifiers 186-188
absolute phrases 38; 69
abstract nouns 15
addresses 38-39
ADJECTIVES 22, 31-32
ADVERBS 23; 186-188
AGREEMENT 72-74; 168-169; 178
APOSTROPHES 49-54; 93-95
apostrophes and personal pronouns 51
appositives 42
articles 45
attributing quotations 43
author's name cited 45
auxiliary verbs 18

B
bibliography 42; 48
books 46
BRACKETS 44

C
Canadian use of commas 37
CAPITALIZATION 175-177
chapters of books 45
chapters and verses 42
CLAUSES 55-67; 90-92
co-ordinate adjectives 37
co-ordinating 24; 37; 41
collective nouns 72
COLONS 42; 81-86
colons and semicolons 133-134
COMMA SPLICES 75-78; 81-89
commands 33
COMMAS 37-39; 81-89; 96-97; 147-148
commas and question marks 36
common nouns 15
comparative adverb form 23
complements 32; 74
complex sentences 62-64
compound adjectives 47; 144-148
compound subject 73
compound numbers 48
compound sentence 59-61; 79-80
compound-complex sentence 65-67
concrete nouns 15
conditional mood 182-185
confirmatory questions 39

CONJUNCTIONS 24; 81-86
conjunctive adverbs 40
consistency 100-101; 170-171
contractions 50; 135-136
contrast 39
correlative 24; 73; 186-188

D
dangling modifiers 126-127
DASHES 43
dates 39
deemphasis 45
definitions 45
demonstrative pronouns 20
dependent clauses 62; 65
DICTION 153-157; 160-164; 172; 179; 180-185
direct quotations 36; 44
direct address 38
doubt 36

E
emphatic tense 30
EXCLAMATION POINTS 36; 132-133
explanatory sentences 42

F
FAN BOYS 24; 37
figures 51
formal quotations 42
fractions 48
FRAGMENTS 114-115; 153-157; 173-174
future perfect 29
future progressive 30
future tense 26-28

G
gerund as noun 16
gerunds 16; 31; 102-106
gerund phrases 68

H
homonyms 47; 179
HYPHENS 47-48

I
indefinite pronouns 21; 72
independent clauses 37; 40; 56; 62; 65; 95-100
infinitive phrases 68
infinitives 31; 102-106
initials 33

interjections 25; 38
interrogative pronouns 21
interruptions 43
intransitive verbs 17
introductory dependent clauses 37; 39
irregular 179
IRREGULAR VERBS 179
italics 46
items in series with commas 41
its and it's (and its') 52-54

J
joint possession 51; 135-138

L
lectures 45
letters 51
linking 17
lists of three or more 41
logic 160-167

M
magazine titles 46
mass nouns 16
measurement 73
misplaced modifiers 125-126
money 73

N
names 38
neither and nor 73
newspapers 46
nonsentences 34
noun complements 74
NOUNS 15; 31
numerals 33

O
object pronouns 10
omission of words 39; 50
omission of periods 34
only 74
or and nor 73
outlines 33

P
paintings 46
PARALLELISM 117-122; 129-131
PARENTHESES 45
parenthetical expressions 38; 43
participle phrases 68
participles 31; 102-106
parts and portions 72

past perfect 29
past progressive 30
past tense 26
PERIODS 33-35
PERSON SHIFTS 100-101; 128-129; 131-132
personal pronouns 20
personal pronouns and apostrophes 51
PHRASES 55; 68-69; 90-92
poems 45
positive adverb form 23
possession, singular 49-50; 135-138
possession, plural 49-50; 135-138
prefixes 47
prepositional phrase included with subject 72
prepositional phrases 68
PREPOSITIONS 25
present perfect 29
present progressive 23
present tense 26
preventing misreading 39
progressive tenses 30
PRONOUN ANTECEDENTS 98-99
pronoun complements 74
PRONOUNS 14; 20-21; 128-129; 139-141
PROOFREADING (general editing)
    123-138; 158-161
proofreading symbols xi-xii
proper nouns 15

Q
QUESTION MARKS 36; 132-133
question marks and periods 35
QUOTATION MARKS and commas 36
quotations and brackets 44
quotations and dashes 43
quotations 38

R
ratios 42
reciprocal pronouns 21
reflexive pronouns 21
regular verbs 18
relative pronouns 17; 20; 74
requests 33
RUN-ONS 76-78; 87-89; 116; 124

S
salutations 39; 42
SEMICOLONS 40-41; 81-86
semicolons and colons 130-134
SENTENCES (also see clauses)
    55-67; 107-112; 144-146
series of words, phrases, clauses 37

shall and will 27-28
shifts (number, person, tense) 131-132
should 28
sic. 46
simple sentences 56-58
single quotation marks 44
song titles 45
SPELLING 153-159; 165-167; 178
statements 33
strong verbs 18-19
subject and verb agreement 72
subject pronouns 20
subordinating conjunctions 24
summarizing statement 43
superlative adverb form 23
suspended compound 47
suspended compound adjectives 47
symbols 51

T

tense shifts 131-132

TENSES 26-30; 162-164; 168-169; 182-185
THE number 73
time 42
titles and subtitles 42; 45-46
to be 74
transitive verbs 17

U

underling (as substitute for italics) 46

V

VERBALS 31-32; 102-106; 149-152
VERBS 17

W

words used in special sense 44

Y

yes and no 38